ALSO BY HILLARY CLINTON

Hard Choices
Living History
An Invitation to the White House
Dear Socks, Dear Buddy
It Takes a Village

Stronger Together

A Blueprint for America's Future

Hillary Clinton
Tim Kaine

Simon & Schuster Paperbacks

New York   London   Toronto   Sydney   New Delhi

Simon & Schuster Paperbacks
An Imprint of Simon & Schuster, Inc.
1230 Avenue of the Americas
New York, NY 10020

First Simon & Schuster trade paperback edition September 2016

For information about special discounts for bulk purchases, please contact Simon & Schuster Special Sales at 1-866-506-1949 or business@simonandschuster.com.

The Simon & Schuster Speakers Bureau can bring authors to your live event. For more information or to book an event contact the Simon & Schuster Speakers Bureau at 1-866-248-3049 or visit our website at www.simonspeakers.com.

Interior design by Hanah Ho, Hillary for America

Manufactured in the United States of America

10 9 8 7 6 5 4 3 2 1

Library of Congress Cataloging-in-Publication Data has been applied for.

ISBN 978-1-5011-6173-5
ISBN 978-1-5011-6174-2 (ebook)

WE HAVE AN OLD-FASHIONED IDEA ABOUT POLITICS:
People who are running to lead the United States of America
should tell you what they're going to do, why they're going to do it, and
how they're going to get it done.

That's what this book is all about. Over the course of this
campaign, we have laid out a comprehensive vision for our country:
building an economy that works for everyone,
not just those at the top; working with our allies and each other to
keep our people safe and our country strong;
and forging a strong sense of American unity to tackle
the problems and seize the opportunities before us.
To that end, we have released more than fifty detailed
policy ideas, on everything from apprenticeships to the Zika virus.
This book adapts the best explanations of those
policy ideas, using language from fact sheets, speeches,
op-eds, and statements we've released over the past fifteen months,
and shares stories from some of the people we've met or who've
written to our campaign.

This is our blueprint for building an America
where we are stronger together.

Contents

Contents

Contents

Contents

On the third day of a bus tour through Pennsylvania and Ohio, July 31, 2016.

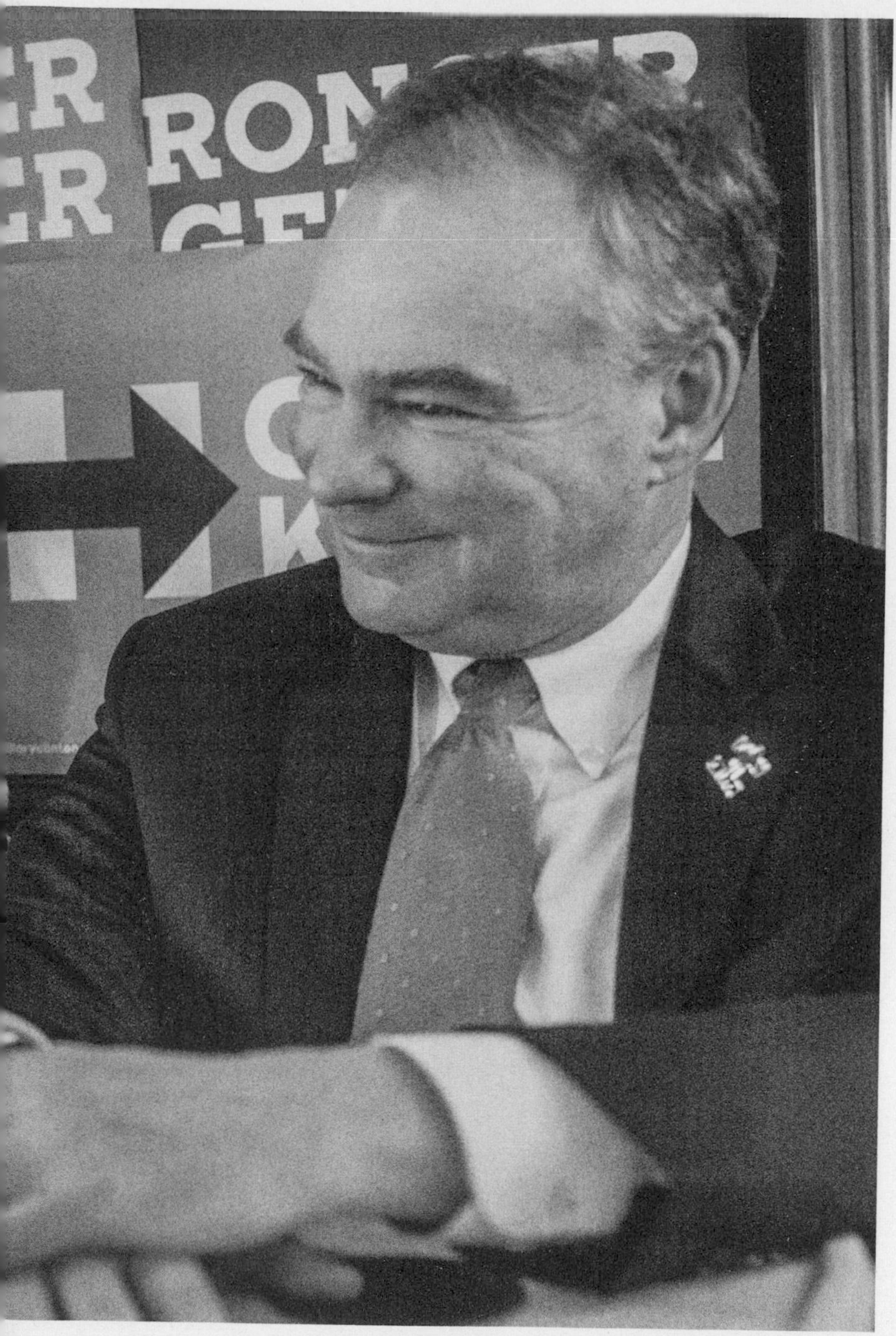

IT HAS BEEN SAID that America is great because America is good.

We agree.

Two hundred and forty years ago, representatives of thirteen colonies met in Philadelphia. We all know the story, but we usually focus our attention on how it turned out—the bold Declaration of Independence, the long war, the drafting of a Constitution that would never have been possible without both painful compromise and an understanding that there would be room for improvement and changes in the future, all of which gave rise to an experiment in self-government that today shines as a beacon of hope for people around the world. We spend less time considering how close we came to never seeing the American story written at all.

From New Hampshire to Georgia, each of the thirteen original colonies had its own customs, its own laws. When they met in Philadelphia, some wanted to stick with the king—and some wanted to stick it to the king.

The revolution—and everything that would follow—hung in the balance. The delegates, many of whom were strangers to each other, some of whom nursed long-held grudges, somehow began to listen to each other, to compromise, to find common purpose.

And by the time they left Philadelphia, they had planted the seed that would grow into a mighty nation. They began to see themselves as one people—stronger together.

America is once again at a moment of reckoning. Powerful forces are threatening to pull us apart. Bonds of trust and respect are fraying. And just as at our founding, there are no guarantees. The future is ours to choose. We have to decide whether we will once again come together and work together so we can all rise together. We have to decide whether we still believe in our nation's motto: E pluribus unum. Out of many, we are one.

Make no mistake—we face our fair share of threats and challenges, and we need to be clear-eyed about them. Our economy is not working the way it should for too many Americans. A lot of people feel there is less and less respect for the work they do—and less respect for them, period.

Our nation is suffering through a quiet epidemic of drug and alcohol addiction. Income and wealth inequality have reached levels not seen since the Roaring Twenties. Children born into the lowest-income families too often stay stuck there as adults, with no chance to fulfill their talents and ambitions.

Our politics have become paralyzed and sometimes poisonous. Instead of protecting Americans' fundamental right to vote, the Supreme Court has protected corporations' right to buy elections. Too many politicians in Washington and in statehouses are more beholden to special interests than they are to the best interests of their constituents.

Our communities have seen horrific mass shootings. We and our allies have come under attack by terrorists. And our long, difficult struggle with racism is still ongoing, with race too often playing a role in who gets ahead and who gets left behind.

But consider the strengths we bring as Americans to meet these challenges. We have the most dynamic and diverse people in the world. We have the most tolerant and generous young people we've ever had. We have the most powerful military and the most innovative entrepreneurs. We have the most enduring values—freedom and equality, justice and opportunity. We should be proud that those words are associated with the United States of America.

Troops on the front lines.
Police officers and firefighters who run toward danger.
Doctors and nurses who care for us. Teachers who change lives.
Entrepreneurs who see possibilities in every problem.
Mothers who lost children to violence
and are building a movement to keep other kids safe . . .

Americans don't say: "I alone can fix it."
We say: "We'll fix it together."

—Hillary, July 28, 2016

Introduction

Love and Kindness—and Action
Hillary Clinton

My grandfather worked in the same Scranton lace mill for fifty years, because he believed that if he gave everything he had, his children would have a better life than he did. And he was right.

My dad, Hugh, made it to college. He played football at Penn State and enlisted in the Navy after Pearl Harbor. When the war was over he started his own small business, printing fabric for draperies. I remember watching him stand for hours over silk screens. He wanted to give my brothers and me opportunities he never had, and he did.

My mother, Dorothy, was abandoned by her parents as a young girl. She ended up on her own at fourteen, working as a housemaid. She was saved by the kindness of others. Her first-grade teacher saw she had nothing to eat at lunch, and brought extra food to share the entire year. The lesson she passed on to me years later stuck with me: No one gets through life alone. We have to look out for each other and lift each other up. And she made sure I learned the words from our Methodist faith: "Do all the good you can, for all the people you can, in all the ways you can, as long as ever you can."

No one gets through life alone.

I grew up in a house filled with opinions. My parents taught me that more than one opinion could live under the same roof—so long as we are committed to listening to each other.

I took the lessons my parents taught me to my first job after law school, at the Children's Defense Fund. I worked as an advocate for children who started life with few chances and plenty of obstacles, just like my mother.

One of my first jobs was going door-to-door in New Bedford, Massachusetts, on behalf of kids with disabilities who were denied the chance to go to school. I still remember meeting a young girl in a wheelchair. We sat on the small back porch of her house, and she told me how badly she wanted to go to school. It just didn't seem possible in those days. And I couldn't stop thinking of my mother and what she'd gone through as a child. It became clear to me that simply caring is not enough. To drive real progress, you have to change both hearts and laws. You need both understanding and action.

It's unusual to hear a candidate for President say we need more love and kindness in our country—but that's exactly what we need. Each of us stumbles at one time or another. I know I've made my share of mistakes and missteps. But life is about how we stand back up—and how we lift each other up, too.

———————

Introduction

Fighting for Right
Tim Kaine

My dad ran a union-organized ironworking shop in the stockyards of Kansas City. And my mom, in addition to all the challenges of raising three sons, was my dad's best saleswoman. That ironworking business was tough. It's the kind of job where you can't cut corners; if you're not careful, you can make one mistake and ruin an awful lot of work in an instant. I learned that working in my dad's shop. My brothers and I all pitched in—because that's what families do.

I went to a Jesuit boys' school with the motto "Men for others." That's what we were taught, and it's where my faith became like my North Star, the organizing principle for what I wanted to do. And that's why I decided to take a year off from law school to volunteer with Jesuit missionaries in Honduras. It turned out that my recently acquired knowledge of constitutional law was pretty useless. But the experience of working in my dad's ironworking shop was actually helpful. So I taught teenagers the basics of carpentry and welding, and they helped me learn Spanish.

In Honduras, I got a firsthand look at a system where a few folks at the top had all the power, and everybody else got left behind. And it convinced me that we have to do everything we can to advance opportunity and equality for everybody, no matter where they come from, how much money they have, what they look like, what accent they have, or who they love.

In 1970, a Republican governor of Virginia, Linwood Holton, believed exactly the same thing. He integrated Virginia's public schools after the state had fought for sixteen years after *Brown v. Board of Education* to keep them segregated. That took political courage. And then he and his wife went even further. They enrolled their own kids, including their daughter Anne, in integrated schools, and it sent a strong signal to the people of Virginia that their governor wasn't going to back down, wasn't going to take half steps, and wasn't going to make rules for others that he wouldn't follow himself.

Many years later, that young girl, Anne, went to law school. Anne and I got married thirty-two years ago at St. Elizabeth Catholic Church, the same parish we still belong to today.

Lin's example helped inspire me to work as a civil rights lawyer representing people who had been turned away from housing either because of the color of their skin or because they were an American with a disability. I did that work for nearly two decades, bringing dozens of lawsuits battling banks, landlords, real estate firms, insurance companies, and even local governments that had treated people unfairly. In 1998, I won a historic verdict against a national insurance company because they had been redlining minority neighborhoods, treating them unfairly in the issuance of homeowner's insurance. At the time I won that case it was the biggest jury verdict ever in a civil rights case in American history. All these years later, I am still striving to do what I did then—to fight for right.

———————

We are each other's countrymen and -women. We share this miraculous country. This land and its heritage is yours, ours, and everyone's who is willing to pledge allegiance and understand the solemn responsibilities of American citizenship. That's what "indivisible" means—that big word that every grade school student knows—that we're in this together, even if that's not always easy.

We face real challenges. But we are not afraid. We will rise to meet them, just as we always have. We will not build a wall. We will not turn our backs on each other or on the world. We will not ban members of a religion from entering our country, or rescind the constitutional principle of birthright citizenship—that if you are born here, you are an American, no matter who your parents are or where they come from. We will not allow dark voices to convince us that it's us against them.

Instead, we will build an economy that works for everyone, not just those at the top, where everyone willing to work hard can find a good job. We will reform our broken campaign finance system and restore access to the ballot box—because we should be protecting people's right to vote, not corporations' right to buy elections. We believe our economy isn't working the way it should because our democracy isn't working the way it should. We will build a path to citizenship for millions of immigrants who are already contributing to our economy. And we will work with all Americans and our allies to fight and defeat terrorism.

The United States needs every one of us to lend our energy, our talents, our ambition to making our nation better and stronger. We should be grateful that of all the world's nations, America is in the best position to build a future of broad prosperity, respectful politics, and advances in medicine, clean energy, and technology that will improve lives—all in a society made stronger by our diversity. That's why "stronger together" is not just a lesson from our history—it's a guiding principle for the nation we are and the future we're going to build.

So let's hold together in the face of our challenges—not turn on each other or tear each other down.

Let's put ourselves in the shoes of police officers, kissing their kids and spouses good-bye every day and heading off to a dangerous job we need them to do.

Let's put ourselves in the shoes of African Americans and Latinos, and try to imagine what it would be like if we had to have "the talk" with our kids about how carefully they need to act every time they're outside of their homes because the slightest wrong move could get them hurt or killed.

And, yes, let's put ourselves in the shoes of those who disagree with us—even those who disagree with us on the causes and the solutions to the challenges we face. Like anyone else, they are trying to figure out their place in a fast-changing America. They want to know how to make a good living and give their kids better futures and opportunities. We need to reclaim the promise of America for everyone—no matter who they vote for.

Let's be more than allies to each other. Let's take on each other's struggles as our own.

*We believe our economy isn't working the way it should because our democracy isn't working the way **it** should.*

We have both built our lives on the conviction that America is stronger together. Our economy is stronger when everyone contributes to it, and everyone can benefit from the work they do. Our communities are stronger when we all pull together to solve our problems and restore our faith in each other. Our country is stronger when we work with our friends and allies to promote peace, prosperity, and security around the world.

Being stronger together doesn't mean everyone will always agree on the best solutions to our problems. We won't. But it does mean that we must all be committed to compromise, to common ground, to finding a path forward together. Debating these questions has always made our country stronger.

None of this is easy. Previous generations have had to overcome difficult challenges. But in the end, if we do the work, we will cease to be divided. We will, in fact, be indivisible with liberty and justice for all.

Stronger Together

1.

GROWING TOGETHER

An Economy that Works for Everyone, Not Just Those at the Top

Rally at Florida International University in Miami, Florida, Saturday, July 23, 2016.

IN 2008, OUR ECONOMY WAS CRATERING. Nearly 9 million people lost their jobs.[1] By 2011, nearly 5 million lost their homes.[2] Thanks to President Obama's leadership and the hard work and resilience of the American people, we have brought our economy back from the brink. We have seeded a revolution in clean energy, slashed our dependence on foreign oil, saved the auto industry, added more than 800,000 manufacturing jobs since the recession's lowest point, and kept the United States at the forefront of technological innovation, from driverless cars to precision medicine.[3]

But we have more work to do. We can't be satisfied with the status quo—not by a long shot. Too many people are living paycheck-to-paycheck, working longer shifts, and taking second and even third jobs just to make ends meet. Too many young people can't buy a first home, start their own business, or even get married because they are weighed

---

1 "Current Employment Statistics," U.S. Department of Labor, Bureau of Labor Statistics, http://www.bls.gov/ces/.
2 Lisa Myers, Rich Gardella and John W. Schoen, "No end in sight to foreclosure quagmire," NBC News, May 9, 2011, http://www.nbcnews.com/id/42881365/ns/business-personal_finance/t/no-end-sight-foreclosure-quagmire/#.V5z1ZfmAOko.
3 "Current Employment Statistics," U.S. Department of Labor, Bureau of Labor Statistics, http://www.bls.gov/ces/.

down by thousands of dollars of student debt. Too many of the wealthiest and big corporations are gaming the system. The super-rich are skipping out on paying their fair share of taxes, and too many companies are shipping jobs overseas to boost profits in the next quarter rather than investing in their workers so they stay profitable for the next decade. And our policies have not kept up with the big changes in the way American families live, learn, and work. We're asking families to rely on an old system of support in a new economic reality.

We can and we will fix these problems. No country is better positioned to thrive in today's global economy. We have the most innovative, enterprising private sector and the most talented workers anywhere in the world.

But first, we need to understand how we got here.

First, too many of our representatives in Washington are in the grips of a failed economic theory called trickle-down economics. It has been proven wrong again and again. But there are still people in Congress who insist on cutting taxes for the wealthy instead of investing in our future.

They careen from one self-inflicted crisis to another—shutting down the government, threatening to default on our national debt, refusing to make the commonsense investments that used to have broad bipartisan support, like rebuilding our roads, bridges, railways, airports, water systems and electric grid, or investing in better education from early childhood through high school and college.

And yes, too many special interests and too many lobbyists have stood in the way of progress while protecting the perks of the privileged few.

It's not just Washington.

Too many corporations have embraced policies that favor hedge funds and other big shareholders and top management at the expense of their workers, communities, and even their long-term value.

While corporate profits are at near-record highs, paychecks for most people have barely budged. Income and wealth inequality in America today has reached levels not seen since the 1920s. Corporate executives are making millions while working families are barely scraping by. The very richest Americans—the top one-tenth of 1 percent—now have nearly as much wealth as the bottom 90 percent.[4] More than four out of ten children born into our lowest-income families never climb out of poverty.[5] Leaders in Washington let Wall Street take big risks with unregulated financial activities, skewed our tax code toward the wealthy, failed to enforce our trade rules, and undermined workers' rights.

A survey of corporate executives found that more than half would hold off making a successful long-term investment if it meant missing a target in the next quarterly earnings report.[6] In another recent survey, more than 60 percent said the pressure to provide short-term returns had increased over the previous five years.[7]

We also know that publicly held companies facing pressure from shareholders are less likely to invest in growth opportunities than their privately held counterparts.[8] American business needs to break free from the tyranny of today's earnings report so they can do what they do best: innovate, invest, and build tomorrow's prosperity.

What if an activist hedge fund had persuaded AT&T to maximize cash flow and close Bell Labs before the transistor or the laser was invented there?

What if Xerox had decided that its Palo Alto research park wasn't doing enough to boost share prices in the short term? A young Steve Jobs would never have visited and the personal computer revolution might not have happened.

What if Congressional budget cuts had shut down DARPA—the Defense Advanced Research Projects Agency—before it developed the early Internet?

The kind of "quarterly capitalism" that dominates today is neither legally required nor economically sound. It's bad for business, bad for wages, and bad for our economy. And fixing it—by rewriting the rules so

---

4 Emmanuel Saez and Gabriel Zucman, "Wealth Inequality in the United States since 1913: Evidence from Capitalized Income Tax Data," 2014, doi:10.3386/w20625.
5 Michael Greenstone, Adam Looney, Jeremy Patashnik, and Muxin Yu, "Thirteen Economic Facts about Social Mobility and the Role of Education," Brookings Institution, June 26, 2013, https://www.brookings.edu/research/thirteen-economic-facts-about-social-mobility-and-the-role-of-education/.
6 John R. Graham, Campbell R. Harvey, and Shiva Rajgopal, "Value destruction and financial reporting decisions," *Financial Analysts Journal* 62, no. 6 (2006), 27–39.
7 Dominic Barton and Mark Wiseman, "Focusing capital on the long term," McKinsey, December 2013, http://www.mckinsey.com/global-themes/leadership/focusing-capital-on-the-long-term.
8 John Asker, Joan Farre-Mensa, and Alexander Ljungqvist, "Corporate Investment and Stock, Market Listing: A Puzzle?", *Review of Financial Studies* (2014): hhu077.

companies treat workers as assets to be invested in rather than costs to be cut, and finally making sure the wealthy, Wall Street, and big corporations pay their fair share in taxes—will be good for everyone.

We have a 70 percent consumption economy. So when only a small share of people see their incomes grow, the vast majority of Americans stay stuck in place. And high inequality compounds the challenges faced by communities that have historically been shut out from fully participating in our economy. For instance, in the immediate aftermath of the recession, white families' net worth remained essentially flat while the net worth of African American families fell by 34 percent.[9] And even though the housing crisis is behind us, roughly one in five African Americans and Latinos face the risk of foreclosure—a much higher proportion than among white Americans.[10]

It's Economics 101: when working people have more money in their pockets, everyone wins. A nurse may finally replace that old car that's broken down one too many times, a teacher will buy the new refrigerator he's been eyeing, and a firefighter will finally go on that hard-earned and much-needed vacation. The businesses they're buying from win because they sell more products and get more revenue. And when they go one step further and raise their employees' wages and give them a share in their hard-earned profits, those workers win, too. That's how a virtuous cycle begins, and each rotation broadens the circle of prosperity. There's more money for everyone—not just those at the top, but those in the middle and those at the bottom, too.

---

9   Rakesh Kochhar and Richard Fry, "Wealth inequality has widened along racial, ethnic lines since end of Great Recession," Pew Research Center, December 12, 2014, http://www.pewresearch.org/fact-tank/2014/12/12/racial-wealth-gaps-great-recession/.
10   Debbie Gruenstein Bocian, Wei Li, and Keith S. Ernst, "Foreclosures by Race and Ethnicity: The Demographics of a Crisis," Center for Responsible Lending, June 18, 2010, http://www.responsiblelending.org/mortgage-lending/research-analysis/foreclosures-by-race-and-ethnicity.pdf.

Share of U.S. adults by income tier

	Lower	Middle	Upper
2015	29%	50%	21%
2011	29	51	20
2001	28	54	18
1991	27	56	17
1981	26	59	15
1971	25	61	14

But when workers don't earn the pay they deserve, a wrench gets thrown in the cycle. And for too long wages have been too low. Most Americans haven't had a raise in fifteen years.[11] When a mother works forty hours a week doing two jobs and still can't support her kids, it's clear that the current federal minimum wage is a starvation wage. Some Americans are doing the same jobs their parents did, but for less pay and fewer benefits. And when you go years without a raise, it can be easy to lose confidence in the future.

That's why creating good-paying jobs is our top priority. We need to make sure that every hardworking American makes enough to support themselves and their family. Raising the federal minimum wage is the right first step. Although Republicans in Congress have blocked us at every step of the way, we're going to keep up the fight—and we'll prevail. In the mean-time, we can look to our states and cities to tackle this challenge. States like New York and California are leading the way, helping millions of working families finally get the wages they deserve. Together, we'll work to replicate their success at the national level.

In addition, there have been big changes in how American fami-lies live, learn, and work, but our policies haven't kept up. There are so many examples of this. Families look a lot different today than they did thirty years ago, and so do our jobs. The movement of women into the workforce has produced enormous economic growth over the past few decades. But with women now the sole or primary breadwinner in a growing number of families, there's more urgency than ever to make it easier for Americans to be good workers, good parents, and good caregiv-ers, all at the same time.[12] We're asking families to rely on an old system of support in a new economic reality. No wonder so many are struggling.

That's why every other advanced economy guarantees paid family leave and earned sick days—because they know that when families are strong, their economies are more stable. Working families need predictable sched-uling, earned sick days and vacation days, quality affordable childcare and health care. These are not luxuries. They're economic necessities.

---

11   "Real Median Household Income in the United States," Federal Reserve, https://fred.stlouisfed.org/series/MEHOINUSA672N.
12   Wendy Wand, Kim Parker, and Paul Taylor, "Breadwinner Moms," Pew, May 2013, http://www.pewsocialtrends.org/2013/05/29/breadwinner-moms/.

As Democrats, we believe our economy should work for everyone, not just those at the top. To make that a reality, we need big, bold, progressive ideas to meet the challenges of today. And we'll measure our success the way our party always has—by how much incomes rise for hardworking families, how many Americans can find good-paying jobs, and how many children can overcome poverty. That's why we will make the boldest investment in good-paying jobs since World War II within the first 100 day; make debt-free college available to all Americans; rewrite the rules so that more companies share profits with employees, and fewer ship profits and jobs overseas; ensure that Wall Street, corporations, and the super-rich pay their fair share; put families first and make sure our policies match how you actually work and live in the twenty-first century.

States without a minimum wage

**Make the boldest investment
in good-paying jobs since World War II
within the first 100 days.**

—

**Make debt-free college available
to all Americans.**

—

**Rewrite the rules so that more companies
share profits with employees,
and fewer ship profits and jobs overseas.**

—

**Ensure that Wall Street, corporations,
and the super-wealthy pay their fair share.**

—

**Put families first and make sure
our policies match how you actually work
and live in the twenty-first century.**

—

**Expand health coverage and tackle mental health,
addiction, and Alzheimer's disease.**

Make the boldest investment in good-paying jobs since World War II within the first 100 days.

Every American should be able to find a job that pays enough to support a family—a good job that provides dignity and a sense of pride.

We know that's possible because we've done it before. After the upheaval of the Great Depression and World War II, our leaders came together to make investments that would help our country prosper for decades. We built highways to connect the entire country, and helped fund college education for returning veterans. We supported our scientists, researchers, and engineers as they opened up entire new fields of human endeavor in medicine, physics, and communications.

Now is the time to be bold and ambitious in building a twenty-first-century economy that benefits everyone, not just those at the top.

We're going to start by proposing, in our first 100 days, the biggest investment in good-paying jobs since World War II. We'll prioritize the kinds of investments in infrastructure, clean energy, small business, and manufacturing that will not only create jobs today, but will build opportunity for decades to come.

That's why, together, we will:

- Invest in our infrastructure to build tomorrow's economy today
- Support manufacturing by launching a plan
  to "Make It In America"
- Empower the job engine of America: our small businesses
- Make America the clean energy superpower
  of the twenty-first century
- Break down barriers for every American by investing
  in communities that have been left behind
- Invest in basic scientific research to open up new
  understanding and create new industries

Invest in our infrastructure to build tomorrow's economy today.

To build a strong economy for the future, we need to start by building infrastructure today. Unfortunately, infrastructure spending has been on a long-term decline—and the consequences are all around us.

As a share of the economy, federal infrastructure investment is roughly half of what it was thirty-five years ago despite broad bipartisan support for infrastructure investment.[13] Estimates of the size of our "infrastructure gap" register in the trillions of dollars.[14] As a result of this shortfall, people can't get to work, congestion keeps commuters stuck in traffic, and airports leave travelers stranded for hours or even days at a time. The impacts of climate change are already being felt across the country, as floods threaten our cities and historic droughts parch the West. Exactly how important it is that we fix our nation's aging infrastructure was made painfully clear by the water crisis in Flint, Michigan, when an entire city was poisoned by incompetence, neglect, and old, outdated pipes. In California, one school district has had to resort to installing Wi-Fi on school buses because so many children lack access to the affordable, high-speed broadband they need to do their homework at home.

This is a national emergency—but it's also a national opportunity. Every dollar of infrastructure investment leads to an estimated $1.60 increase in GDP the following year—and twice that over the subsequent twenty years.[15] That's because investing in infrastructure ultimately puts more money in workers' pockets to spend at local restaurants, shops, and movie theaters. And every $1 billion in infrastructure spending creates 13,000 jobs, according to the White House Council of Economic Advisers.

---

13 Elizabeth Mcnihol, "It's Time for States to Invest in Infrastructure," Center on Budget and Policy Priorities, February 2016, http://www.cbpp.org/research/state-budget-and-tax/its-time-for-states-to-invest-in-infrastructure.

14 "Report Card for America's Infrastructure," American Society of Civil Engineers, March 2013, http://infra structurereportcard.org/a/documents/2013-Report-Card.pdf.; and Rosabeth Moss Kanter, *Move: Putting America's Infrastructure Back in the Lead* (2015).

15 Isabelle Cohen, Thomas Freiling, and Eric Robinson, "The Economic Impact and Financing of Infrastructure Spending," College of William & Mary Thomas Jefferson Program in Public Policy Williamsburg, December 2011, https://www.wm.edu/as/publicpolicy/documents/prs/aed.pdf.

As projects get completed, businesses realize savings as they ship goods. Better-designed transit systems connect more people to jobs and economic opportunities that were all but impossible to reach before. And new investments in twenty-first-century technology—like smarter, more resilient electric grids, safer and more sustainable water infrastructure, and high-speed broadband—help improve public health and safety, save families and cities money, and open up new economic opportunities.

That's why in our first one hundred days we will deliver the most ambitious investment in our nation's infrastructure since President Eisenhower built the Interstate Highway System. Our plan will include significant new public investment, as well as a new National Infrastructure Bank to leverage private capital from investors and pension funds. We want these investments to be built to last. That's why we will prioritize resilient infrastructure built to withstand the projected impacts of climate change. And we will prioritize making investments that upgrade and expand multiple kinds of infrastructure at once. Broadband cable can be laid at the same time a water system or gas pipes are being upgraded, for instance. An improved airport can have an even greater economic impact if transit options are built to make it easier for travelers to get there. We need to align our project planning and investments to make these kinds of "multi-modal" projects more common.

When President Eisenhower asked Congress to fund a national highway system, he recognized that "more than any single action by the government since the end of the war, this one would change the face of America." He was right. We will focus these additional resources on investments that will change the face of our country for the better and build a strong twenty-first-century economy.

We will focus on:

- **Connecting every household to affordable broadband and leading the world in next-generation wireless technology.** By 2020, we want every household in America to be able to access affordable, high-speed broadband. We need to put Wi-Fi in more schools, workplaces, libraries, hospitals, and other public spaces, so Americans can get online no matter where they are.

And we'll lead the world in deploying the next generation of wireless technologies that will make the "Internet of Things" possible.

- **Building the transportation systems of tomorrow.** Crumbling roads and "structurally deficient" bridges are some of the most urgent and obvious signs of our infrastructure needs, and we will repair them. But we also need to make smart investments in building more modern roads and bridges, and revitalize our airports and transit. We will fund research into high-tech, Internet-enabled transportation technologies, like a wide-ranging system of advanced energy fueling stations for the twenty-first-century fleet; a network of roadway sensors that will alert drivers to an accident or a dangerous icy patch a mile ahead; and vehicles that can sense and communicate with one another, saving lives and reducing traffic. We will also complete the NextGen national airspace system, which will improve communication and reduce delays across our air travel network.

  Although transit ridership has grown dramatically across the country, investment has not kept pace with demand. Chronic underinvestment in transit disproportionately hurts low-income communities and communities of color, as a lack of transportation options can make it much harder for people to get to work and school. We will encourage cities to work with low-income communities to ensure new transit investments are being made in a way that increases access for those who need it most.

- **Making America a clean energy superpower.** Our electric grid is stuck in the past, and families and businesses are the ones who pay the price. We need to upgrade it with smart grid technologies that reduce energy costs and give consumers more energy options, like rooftop solar panels. Our goal is to have half a billion solar panels installed by the end of our first term. We need to accelerate our transition to a clean energy economy so we can get half our electricity from clean, zero-carbon sources within a decade, and start building the transmission lines and storage technologies that will make that possible.

- **Eliminating "choke points" of commerce to save businesses and consumers money.** Every year, our businesses have to spend an extra $27 billion in transportation costs just because of congestion in our freight networks.[16] A cargo train can reach Chicago from the West Coast within two days, only to spend as much as thirty hours getting across Chicago itself.[17] These delays are costly for farmers, manufacturers, small businesses, and consumers alike. We need to make major, coordinated investments to eliminate these "choke points" of commerce, saving money and making our entire economy more competitive.

- **Revitalizing public schools in every zip code.** We need safe, healthy, high-tech public schools in every zip code so all of our kids can get the education they deserve. It's unacceptable that today kids in Detroit are sitting in classrooms that are infested with mold and rodents. Kids in Newark can't drink the water because it contains dangerous levels of lead. And that's nothing to say of all the schools where science labs are outdated or budget cuts have closed libraries. In fact, one survey found that 53 percent of public schools need extensive repair or replacement.[18] We will finally make these much-needed renovations.

- **Rebuilding our water systems to protect public health.** Parts of our drinking water system are more than a century old, and the system as a whole leaks nearly 6 billion gallons of water a day—that's roughly one-sixth of our national daily water use. Old, overburdened wastewater systems send more than 900 billion gallons of untreated sewage a year into our rivers and streams.[19] And in the West, record droughts and raging wildfires

---

16   "An Economic Analysis of Transportation Infrastructure Investment," The White House Council of Economic Advisers, July 2014, https://www.whitehouse.gov/sites/default/files/docs/economic_analysis_of_transportation_investments.pdf.
17   "About Create," Chicago Region Environmental and Transportation Efficiency Program, http://www.create program.org/about.htm.
18   "Condition of America's Public School Facilities: 2012–2013," U.S. Department of Education, 2014, http://nces.ed.gov/pubs2014/2014022.pdf.
19   Ben Bovarnick, Shiva Polefka, and Arpita Bhattacharyya, "Rising Water, Rising Threat," Center for American Progress, October 2014, https://cdn.americanprogress.org/wp-content/uploads/2014/10/wastewater-report.pdf.

are destroying land, depleting reservoirs, and straining budgets. To solve these problems, we will harness both public and private resources to revitalize our aging water infrastructure, expand innovative efforts to capture and reuse water, and increase federal investment in water conservation in the West. And we will establish the first-ever national Water Innovation Lab to pioneer advances in water technology, just as our existing national labs have done for energy.

Revitalizing manufacturing by launching a plan to "Make It In America."

Manufacturing matters. Manufacturing jobs pay well and provide workers with security, dignity, and a path to the middle class. The industry is not only the backbone of our economy but also improves our national security, and makes American innovators more competitive.

And after many years of manufacturing decline, there's finally some good news: Assembly lines are rolling again across America. Exports have increased by more than 40 percent since President Obama took office.[20] American companies have retooled and expanded last century's factories to meet this century's challenges. In Michigan, the same facilities that used to churn out B-24 bombers will be rolling out driverless cars. Chevy is making electric vehicles using union labor—and powering the factory with clean energy. Companies are using new technology to create stronger steel, weave tougher fabrics, and make thinner, stronger glass right here in America. American exports total more than $2 trillion a year—and exporters pay workers higher wages than other businesses.[21]

But we need to do more. We need to invest in building regional manufacturing hubs and supporting our workforce to make our communities the first choice for industrial production from steel, cars, and aircraft to clean energy technologies. We won't let anyone tell us we can't make things in America anymore—we can and we will.

That's why we will:

- **Establish "Make It In America Partnerships" to harness our country's regional strengths**. We will build new partnerships that link together workers, unions, businesses, universities, and government at all levels to build on regional strengths in particular industries and encourage industries to locate there and create jobs. The partnership approach will help new ideas move

---

20 "Global Patterns of U.S. Merchandise Trade," International Trade Administration, 2009–2015.
21 "US International Trade in Goods and Services—May 2016," U.S. Census Bureau, Bureau of Economic Analysis, https://www.census.gov/foreign-trade/Press-Release/current_press_release/ft900.pdf.

from university labs to factory floors, support smaller manufacturers by helping them participate in regional supply chains, and create more good-paying jobs across the country. This approach is already being piloted in places like Youngstown, Ohio, where a public-private coalition of partners from industry, government, and academia have formed America Makes, which is advancing 3-D printing and additive manufacturing technologies across a range of industries.

- **Make American manufacturing the cleanest and most competitive in the world.** We will set a goal to improve energy efficiency by one-third within ten years, saving American companies more than $50 billion every year.[22] And we will ensure that American leadership in producing some of the lowest-carbon steel, aluminum, glass, and other materials is recognized and rewarded in public and private procurement by creating a new "Buy Clean" product labeling system.

- **Revitalize the hardest-hit manufacturing communities with new investment.** When a factory closes its doors, entire communities suffer. Without new investments to bring back jobs, we often see a downward spiral of layoffs, foreclosures, underinvestment—all of which lead to chronic blight and neglect. That's why we will create a new Manufacturing Renaissance Tax Credit to attract new capital, business, and jobs; establish a zero capital gains option on long-term investments; and provide tax relief for renovating, refurbishing, or repurposing plants.

- **Invest in our manufacturing workforce.** To win the global competition for manufacturing jobs, we need to harness the skills and talents of our workforce. We will encourage the expansion of proven, high-quality training and apprenticeship programs that enable workers to earn while they learn, including through

---

22 Calculation based on Energy Information Administration data.

a new tax credit for every apprentice hired. We will expand nationwide credentialing efforts, which help workers gain recognition and compensation for their skills. And we will build on successful models that allow federal student aid to be used for high-quality career and technical training programs that help raise incomes and increase skills.

Empower the job engine of America:
our small businesses.

Small but mighty, America's small businesses create nearly two-thirds of new jobs, drive innovation, and help hardworking entrepreneurs provide a middle-class life for their families.

America is meant to be a place where anyone with a good idea and the willingness to do the hard work of seeing it through can build a successful business. That enterprising spirit helped build the strongest economy in the world. Harnessing that spirit for the twenty-first century will require extending opportunity to every American, no matter their race, gender, or background, to build a business, realize a dream, and support their family.

But all too often there are barriers holding hardworking Americans back. For too many aspiring small business owners it's still too hard to get an idea off the ground. Uneven regulatory and licensing requirements make it tough to expand. And credit is still far too hard to come by.

Small business owners and entrepreneurs need access to financing and credit to build, expand, and hire more Americans. Lending has recovered since the crisis, but it's still hard for new firms to get credit. A Federal Reserve Survey found that the current market is especially hard for the smallest firms and start-ups. And more than half of small businesses face payment delays, which can cause serious cash-flow problems and hold back small businesses from being able to invest in new inventory, expand their production, or even meet payroll.[23]

And despite the fact that millions more women have opened businesses and become their own bosses in recent years, they're still starting out with about half the financial capital compared to their male counterparts and are still less likely to run their own businesses.[24] Like women, Latinos and African Americans start their small businesses with

---

23 Amy Feldman, "Federal Reserve Survey Of Small Business Credit: Higher Approval Rates, But Many Still See Shortfall," *Forbes*, March 3, 2016, http://www.forbes.com/sites/amyfeldman/2016/03/03/federal-reserve-survey-small-business-financing-approval-rates-higher-but-many-still-face-gap/#7fac90c84245; and Anna Eschenburg, "Small Businesses Wait on Late Payments," *Fundbox*, November 2015, https://fundbox.com/blog/late-payments/.
24 Michael Barr, "Minority and Women Entrepreneurs: Building Capital, Networks, and Skills," The Hamilton Project, March 2015, http://www.hamiltonproject.org/assets/legacy/files/downloads_and_links/minority_women_entrepreneurs_building_skills_barr_final.pdf.

roughly half the capital a white male would typically have access to.[25] In many cases, these entrepreneurs do not even apply for loans because they are afraid of being rejected.[26] More dreams die in the parking lots of banks than anywhere else.

Not only is that unacceptable, but it could actually hurt economic growth and hinder economic opportunities for too many Americans. According to research, women- and minority-owned small businesses saw far faster growth of sales, receipts, and values of shipments than other small businesses. Moreover, researchers have found that by starting their own businesses, women and minority Americans can reduce gender and racial wealth gaps with white men.[27] By supporting American small business owners and entrepreneurs, we can build ladders of opportunity for them and their families.

That's why we will:

- **Cut red tape that holds back small businesses and entrepreneurs.** Right now, it takes longer to start a small business in the United States than it does in Canada, South Korea, or France.[28] That's not right. We will simplify our overly complicated federal regulations and work with states to remove barriers that make it too hard to get a small business off the ground.

- **Expand access to capital.** Small businesses need financing and credit to build, grow, expand, and hire. But the smallest firms and start-ups struggle the most to access the credit they need to open their doors. And on average, women small business owners start out with just half the capital men do. That's why we will expand federal funding for loans, training, and mentoring for small businesses. And we will double the Community Development Financial Institutions Fund, which supports organizations that provide between 65 and 90 percent of loans to

25 Ibid.
26 Ibid.
27 Ibid.
28 "Doing Business Project," World Bank, http://data.worldbank.org/indicator/IC.REG.DURS.

historically underserved small business owners, so we can help even more entrepreneurs get started.

- **Expand access to new markets.** Every small business should be able to tap new markets, whether they are on the other side of the state, the country, or the world. That's why we will invest in our infrastructure and work to harness the power of the Internet to help more small businesses find new customers. And we will stand up for American workers by supporting the Export-Import Bank and other policies that drive American exports.

- **Provide tax relief and simplification.** Small businesses with one to five employees spend an average of 150 hours and $1,100 per employee in order to comply with federal taxes— twenty times higher than the average for bigger companies.[29] We will provide tax relief and simplification for small businesses so they can focus on what they do best: expanding their companies and hiring more Americans. And we will reduce the capital gains tax rate to zero for qualified small business stock held for more than five years.

---

29   Martin A. Sullivan, testimony before Joint Economic Committee of the U.S. Congress, April 15, 2015, http://www.jec.senate.gov/public/_cache/files/bbad3a40-6b0d-4586-a37e-7d8a08d80fbc/marty.pdf.

Make America the clean-energy superpower
of the twenty-first century.

Climate change is an urgent threat to our economy, our national security, and the health and safety of our communities. Already, American families are seeing the impacts of climate change with their own eyes, from the historic drought in California to more frequent floods in cities like Miami and Annapolis to region-wide weather events like Superstorm Sandy. And we know these impacts are only going to get worse, with longer summers, more frequent heat waves, increasingly severe downpours, fiercer wildfire seasons, rising sea levels contributing to bigger storm surges—and serious consequences for our economy and our public health. The latest science suggests that global sea levels could rise as much as six feet by the end of the century, affecting millions of Americans and billions of dollars of coastal property, if we do not change the way we do business and cut carbon pollution and other greenhouse gas emissions sharply. To avoid the worst effects of climate change and avoid leaving our children to inherit a planet that is damaged beyond repair, we need to accelerate the transition to a clean energy economy and sharply reduce the greenhouse gas pollution that causes global warming.

We have made progress. U.S. carbon pollution has been cut to its lowest level since 1995.[30] We get three times as much energy from the wind and thirty times as much from the sun as we did in 2008.[31] And using cleaner energy has helped prevent thousands of asthma attacks and hundreds of premature deaths. But we need to do more to protect public health by meeting America's carbon pollution reduction goals and compete and win in the $13.5 trillion market for investment in clean energy and advanced vehicles.[32] That is why we will get started on day one, and not wait for climate deniers and defeatists in Congress to take action. Not only will we meet the pledge President Obama made in Paris to cut greenhouse gas emissions by 26 to 28 percent below 2005 levels

30 "Inventory of U.S. Greenhouse Gas Emissions and Sinks, 1990-2014," U.S. Environmental Protection Agency, https://www3.epa.gov/climatechange/Downloads/ghgemissions/US-GHG-Inventory-2016-Chapter-2-Trends.pdf.
31 Calculations based on Energy Information Administration data.
32 "Climate pledges for COP21 slow energy sector emissions growth dramatically," International Energy Agency, October 2015, https://www.iea.org/newsroomandevents/pressreleases/2015/october/climate-pledges-for-cop21-slow-energy-sector-emissions-growth-dramatically.html.

by 2025, we will seek to exceed it by transforming our energy system, pioneering cleaner transportation options, making American manufacturing the cleanest and most competitive in the world, and making our homes and buildings more energy efficient. We are committed to keeping global temperature increases below the 2 degrees Celsius threshold, and will pursue policies to cut emissions 80 percent by mid-century.

To make America the clean-energy superpower of the twenty-first century, we will:

- **Generate enough renewable energy to power every home in America.** Our goal is to have 500 million solar panels installed within four years—the equivalent of installing rooftop solar on over 25 million homes—and to generate enough renewable energy to power every home in America within a decade. We'll harness as much as twelve gigawatts of clean energy by installing powerhouses on existing dams owned by the Army Corps of Engineers—enough energy to power Alaska, Delaware, Maine, New Hampshire, and Vermont combined.[33] And we'll turn America's public lands and waters into engines of the clean energy economy by expanding clean energy generation tenfold. All together, we'll add more energy to our grid than in any previous decade, just by expanding renewables, and get half of our electricity from clean, zero-carbon energy sources within ten years. And we will support additional clean energy research and development in advanced materials, battery storage, carbon capture and sequestration, and other areas—because climate change is too important a challenge to take any potential solution off the table.

- **Launch a Clean Energy Challenge for states, cities, and rural communities.** Smart federal standards and goals are important, but much of our energy policy gets decided at the regional,

---

33   "Non-Powered Dam Resource Assessment," U.S. Department of Energy, http://nhaap.ornl.gov/content/non-powered-dam-potential. Calculations based on Energy Information Administration data.

state, and city level, and that's where we are seeing the boldest action to tackle climate change. Cities like Cincinnati are buying 100 percent clean energy. Rural electric co-ops from Colorado coal country to Wisconsin dairy communities are investing in solar power. In fact, twenty-nine states now have renewable portfolio standards which require them to increase energy production from renewable sources.[34] We will launch a new Clean Energy Challenge to partner with states, cities, and rural communities that are ready to lead on clean energy, with competitive grants, Solar X-Prizes for cutting red tape and expanding rooftop solar opportunities to low-income families, and dedicated programs to expand clean energy and energy efficiency in rural communities.

- **Invest in energy efficiency to save families, businesses, and government money.** Buildings consume more energy than any other single sector, accounting for 40 percent of demand and costing families and businesses almost $400 billion per year.[35] Taxpayers spend more than $50 billion annually on energy in public buildings—more than the budgets of NASA, the National Science Foundation, the Department of Commerce, and the EPA combined.[36] Inefficient buildings not only raise energy costs and increase pollution, they are less healthy to live in and less productive to work in. We will set a national goal of cutting energy waste in homes, schools, stores, municipal buildings, hospitals, and offices by one-third within ten years, using better building codes, stronger efficiency standards, and new incentives. Achieving this goal will cut energy costs by $600 for the average American household and save taxpayers more than $8 billion a year.[37]

---

34 "State Renewable Portfolio Standards and Goals," National Conference of State Legislatures, July 2016, http://www.ncsl.org/research/energy/renewable-portfolio-standards.aspx.
35 "Building Energy Performance Policy," Institute for Market Information, http://www.imt.org/policy/building-energy-performance-policy.
36 Unlocking American Efficiency," United Technologies and Rhodium Group, May 2013, http://naturalleader.com/wp-content/uploads/2016/04/RHG_UnlockingAmericanEfficiency_May2013-v4.pdf.
37 Calculation based on Energy Information Administration data.

- **Build modern energy infrastructure to power our economy.** We typically don't think about where our energy comes from—a light goes on when we flip the switch, our car starts when we turn the key in the ignition, our house gets warmer or cooler when we adjust the thermostat, and we go about our lives. In fact, where we get the energy for those everyday tasks—and how much we need—has changed dramatically in recent years, thanks to big gains in renewable energy, a boom in domestic oil and gas production, and historic advances in energy efficiency. But our policies and infrastructure have not kept pace with the times, and we need to build a twenty-first-century energy infrastructure that enables the clean energy economy we want to build. That means we need to modernize pipelines, including thousands of miles of natural gas pipelines that leak methane beneath our cities, and oil pipelines that can lead to toxic spills. We need to improve rail safety and protect communities from dangerous rail car explosions. And we need to build a smarter, more secure, modern electric grid that takes full advantage of new renewable energy resources and is resilient to extreme weather and cyberattack.

- **Ensure safe and responsible natural gas production.** We need to do more to make natural gas production safer and more responsible. We will put in place tough standards to cut methane emissions that contribute to climate change from both new and existing sources. We will close the Halliburton loophole and protect drinking water. We will work to reduce the risk of seismic activity from oil and gas production. And if a state or local community decides they don't want to allow production to take place, we will stand with them.

**Break down barriers for every American by investing
in communities that have been left behind.**

Flint, Michigan, is a city of 99,000 people—56 percent African
American, four in ten living below the poverty line—that spent nearly
two years drinking poisoned water.[38]

As a result, thousands of kids were exposed to harmful levels of lead,
which can irreparably harm brain development and cause learning and
behavioral problems.

But the problems in Flint go beyond the lead in the water. Years of
underinvestment in the city created a hollowed-out community without
enough jobs or opportunity for the people who live there. Not enough
families have access to the quality education their children deserve. And
the people of Flint have too little political power, which left them vulnerable to harm and indifference. For the two years that Flint was living
with poisoned water, residents' concerns were downplayed and ignored
by the state government.

There are too many Flints in this country—too many places where
overwhelmingly low-income communities and communities of color face
chronic pollution, exposure to toxic chemicals, and staggering neglect.
From Flint to Albuquerque, Baltimore to El Paso, Cleveland to Chicago,
there are still opportunity deserts—parts of cities, towns, and rural communities that have been cut off from jobs, investment, and, all too often,
hope. It's time for that to change.

The hard truth is that we still face a complex set of economic, social, and political challenges as a nation. It is not enough to create jobs
if we do not also take on the reality of systemic racism. It is not enough
to transition to a clean energy future if we let the coal communities that
kept our lights on for generations sit in the dark. These challenges are
intersectional, mutually reinforcing, and we have to take on all of them.

---

38 "Quick Facts: Flint City, Michigan," U.S. Census Bureau, http://www.census.gov/quickfacts/table/
PST045215/2629000,00.

We'll start addressing them by:

- **Breaking down barriers for communities of color.** People of color face disproportionately high barriers to starting a small business, buying a home, and even getting to a job. For instance, African Americans and Latinos tend to have about half the capital of white men when they start a business—and that gap actually widens as their businesses mature. We will provide mentoring, training, and access to small business incubators to 50,000 entrepreneurs in underserved communities and expand federal funding to support small businesses. We will support initiatives in underserved communities to match up to $10,000 in savings for responsible homeowners who earn less than the area median income to put toward a down payment on a first home. And we will create a new "Infrastructure to Opportunity" fund to make the kinds of investments that better connect people to opportunity, including better transit systems, high-speed broadband, and safer, healthier schools.

- **Honoring our Tribal communities.** We will begin by honoring the trust and treaty responsibilities of the U.S. government. The Native American unemployment rate is nearly double the national average.[39] Too many Native youth don't feel like they really matter to America. With over 40 percent of the Native community under the age of twenty-four, we know that investing in Native American youth is a critical step toward building strong communities and spurring economic revitalization.[40] We will continue to support the Generation Indigenous program that has made important strides in promoting new investments and increased engagement with Native American youth. We will empower Tribal governments to help their own citizens combat

---

39 Katherine Peralta, "Native Americans Left Behind in the Economic Recovery," *U.S. News and World Report,* November 27, 2014, http://www.usnews.com/news/articles/2014/11/27/native-americans-left-behind-in-the-economic-recovery.
40 "Indian Country Demographics," National Congress of American Indians, http://www.ncai.org/about-tribes/demographics, accessed July 2016.

drug and alcohol addiction by implementing preventive programming, investing in treatment and recovery, and ensuring that all first responders have access to naloxone.

- **Building a bright future for coal communities.** For generations, America's coal communities kept our lights on and our factories humming. But employment in coal mining has been on the decline for decades, and layoffs have increased as the United States gets more energy from cleaner sources, like natural gas and renewable energy. Just as we are committed to tackling climate change, we are committed to making sure America's coal communities remain a vital part of our economic future. We will make sure coal workers and their families get the benefits they've earned and the respect they deserve by protecting health care and pensions. And we are prepared to invest billions in building a strong future for coal country, by building new infrastructure, repurposing abandoned mine lands and power plants to host new businesses, expanding and simplifying the New Markets Tax Credit to attract more private investment to coal country, and creating a Coal Communities Challenge Fund to support locally driven economic development priorities in areas like small business development, health care, housing, clean energy, and tourism.

- **Supporting youth jobs.** Roughly one in ten Americans between the ages of sixteen and twenty-four is unemployed, more than twice the national average.[41] And these numbers hide devastating racial disparities: the unemployment rate for African American teenagers is almost twice that of white teenagers, while the unemployment rate for Latino teenagers is roughly a quarter higher. Being unemployed at a young age can have a permanent "scarring effect" as a person ages, contributing to lower wages and longer periods of unemployment later in life. We will create

---

41 "(Seas) Unemployment Rate—16–24 yrs," U.S. Department of Labor, Bureau of Labor Statistics, July 2016, http://data.bls.gov/timeseries/LNS14024887?include_graphs=false&output_type=column&years_option=all_years.

millions of jobs for young people in hard-hit communities through new grant programs and partnerships; invest in "opportunity youth," the approximately 2.3 million young people who are neither in work nor in school, by expanding successful jobs and skills programs; and expand high-quality apprenticeship programs that provide young people an opportunity to earn a paycheck while they learn valuable skills.[42]

- **Investing in rural America.** Forty-six million people live in rural America, but too many rural communities struggle with high levels of poverty and unemployment, and lack access to health care and affordable education.[43] We will invest in the next generation of family farms, expand access to capital for rural small businesses, invest in biofuels and other clean energy solutions, and support new advances in telemedicine that will help rural communities get more timely health care.

- **Target more investment to communities left out and left behind.** Some communities and neighborhoods struggle with generational poverty, decade after decade, in which those born into poverty stay there throughout their lives. To increase public and private investment in these hardest-hit communities, we will explore policies like South Carolina Representative Jim Clyburn's 10-20-30 proposal, in which 10 percent of program dollars are directed to communities where 20 percent or more of the population has been living in poverty for 30 years or longer. We will also expand and simplify the New Markets Tax Credit, which has successfully steered billions in private investment for economic development activities, so more communities can benefit.

---

42   YouthBuild.org, https://www.youthbuild.org/about-youthbuild, accessed July 2016.
43   "Overview," U.S. Department of Agriculture, Economic Research Service, http://www.ers.usda.gov/topics/rural-economy-population/population-migration.aspx.

Invest in basic scientific research to open up new understanding and create new industries.

Pushing beyond the boundaries of what we know is core to who we are as Americans. It's what pushed us to send astronauts to the moon and sequence the human genome. It's what has driven us to invest in cutting-edge technologies and push forward to discover treatments for diseases that were once death sentences. And it's what will change the trajectory of our future.

We live in a time of incredible scientific and technological accomplishment—and even greater promise—from advances in clean energy to breakthroughs in medicine to greater exploration in space. The federal government plays a critical role in shaping the agenda of research and development in America and around the world. For example, the Human Genome Project started as an idea a few academic biologists had to analyze DNA. That simple idea grew into one of the greatest federal investments and largest collaborative biology projects in scientific history. In 1988, Congress funded the NIH to launch the project and work with researchers around the world. Fifteen years later, they had successfully sequenced the human genome—and with it, they laid the groundwork for innovative new medical treatments, groundbreaking research, and entire new industries. Sequencing a single genome cost $100 million in 2001 and took the full resources of the federal research system; by 2015, the cost was only about $1,000. That's the power of research.

That's why we need to do everything we can to fund the basic scientific and medical research that advances human knowledge—and can even create entire new industries.

Climate change—a defining challenge of our time—is one issue that needs greater government investment. It threatens our economy, our national security, and our children's health and future. We need to move urgently to save the only planet we've got. We are on the cusp of great advances in clean energy, but too many projects still need more funding in the lab or in the field. We will increase public investment in both basic and applied research to develop new technologies and attract new private investment.

To be a leader in clean energy globally, we need to create more public-private collaborations abroad, such as the U.S.-China Clean Energy Research Center. This partnership was set up in 2009 and is funded by governments, academic institutions, and private corporations—increasing foreign companies' investments in clean energy.[44] We will use this framework to lead an even greater push for global technology development.

We can structure these investments like those in the biomedical field, which receive extensive private-sector capital in part due to sustained public funding. In the last several years, government investments have spurred discoveries in mapping genes, treating HIV/AIDS, and preventing less well-known—but no less devastating—diseases. President Obama has made significant efforts to ramp up medical innovation, from the Precision Medicine and BRAIN initiatives to Vice President Biden's effort to accelerate cancer research.

We will build on these efforts to accelerate the pace of medical progress, ensuring that we invest in our scientists and give them the resources they need to invigorate study in the life sciences and to make progress against the full range of diseases. We will make even greater investments in the National Institutes of Health that are not only significant in size but are predictable year-after-year, providing greater certainty for principal investigators and greater opportunity for aspiring physicians and scientists. We will make sure investments span the full spectrum of research, from basic research to translational and clinical research, and ensure that data is shared. It is important that we do everything we can to get more scientists working together to generate new knowledge and use it to prevent and treat diseases more effectively.

Our investment in research will expand beyond clean energy and medicine. For instance, NASA's achievements in science, technology, and exploration help us better understand our universe and inspire and educate generations of young people in this country to pursue careers in science. Space exploration is a reminder that our capacity for curiosity is limitless—and may be matched only by our ability to achieve great things if we work together. NASA also conducts vital research in aero-

---

44   "U.S.-China Clean Energy Cooperation," U.S. Department of Energy, January 2011, http://www.us-china-cerc.org/pdfs/US_China_Clean_Energy_Progress_Report.pdf.

nautics and earth sciences, and supports critical data and analysis used by scientists around the world to understand climate change.

We will strengthen support for NASA and work in partnership with the international scientific community to launch new missions to space, including pursuing the long-term goal of human exploration of Mars. As the only nation to have landed astronauts on the surface of the moon, the United States is uniquely suited to lead the international effort to make manned missions to Mars possible. Over the decades, NASA technologies have made possible the growth of private industries in everything from satellite communications to the SpaceX rockets that ferry astronauts and supplies to the International Space Station. We will explore ways to further leverage NASA's strengths and foster more collaboration between the agency and innovative, technology-oriented companies that create jobs and foster growth across the economy.

We will also expand funding for other key agencies that support and conduct groundbreaking research, from the National Science Foundation to the National Institute of Standards and Technology to DARPA, all of which will continue to play a vital role in pushing the boundaries of our knowledge and creating the good-paying jobs of the future.

Make debt-free college available to all Americans.

Education is the key to so much we want to achieve as a country:
A stronger, more equitable economy; a healthier, more vibrant democracy;
a future in which we meet challenges with ingenuity and skill. Education
is also the key to our young people achieving their dreams. It's how they
discover their passions, develop their talents, and start their journey
toward fulfilling and challenging careers. That's why the strength of our
country depends on the ability of every American to access a quality
education—no matter how much money they have.

College used to be affordable, but for too many Americans the
promise of a college education is out of reach. Families sending their
children to public colleges and universities have watched tuition balloon
by 40 percent over the last ten years alone, even as family incomes have
remained flat. In part, that's because states have been cutting spending
on higher education, and colleges have responded not by tightening
their belts but by raising tuition. If we want to build an America where
every child can achieve their dreams, this has to change.

While we work to make college affordable, we must address the
crisis of student debt. Over the last ten years total student debt in our
economy has more than doubled and now exceeds $1.2 trillion.
Nearly seven out of every ten new college graduates are in debt, and

these graduates carry an average of roughly $30,000 in student loans. Student debt has surpassed credit card debt, car loan debt, and home equity lines of credit to be the second-largest source of consumer debt. This is not just an issue for borrowers: It's hurting our entire economy. Student debt prevents Americans from starting families, buying homes, and launching small businesses.

Stacy went to the University of New Hampshire and recently earned a master's degree in education. She wants to be a social studies teacher. But when she applies for jobs, she's told she needs more experience. So she's underemployed, owes thousands in student loans, and is still living with her parents and driving an old, unsafe car that she can't afford to replace. Stacy and countless other young people like her are worried their lives will never really start because they are carrying so much student debt.

And here's something we don't say nearly often enough: College is crucial, but a four-year degree should not be the only path to a good-paying job. Later, we will discuss our plan to expand high-quality apprenticeship programs so more people can learn a skill, practice a trade, and make a good living doing it. We also need to expand technical education in high schools, make community college free, and expand high-quality nontraditional credentialing and training programs.

If we want to create an economy that works for everyone, not just those at the top, we need to take bold and decisive action to make college affordable and relieve the crushing burden of student debt. Students and families are ready to do their part. Everyone else—the federal government, states, and colleges and universities—needs to step up and do theirs. It's time to make a New College Compact with every American: costs won't be a barrier, and debt won't hold you back.

To create a debt-free future for America's graduates, the New College Compact will:

- Make debt-free college a reality, and promote college affordability
- Help young people break free from the crushing burden of student debt
- Crack down on predatory schools, lenders, and bill collectors
- Launch "Let's Start Something" to allow young entrepreneurs to defer their federal student loans while they get their ventures off the ground

College completion rates for students who enroll

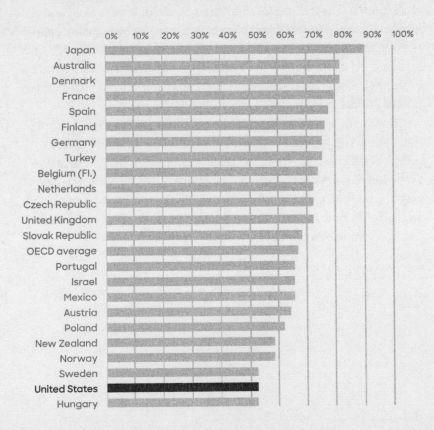

Make debt-free college a reality for every American.

Imagine an America where we tackle the runaway costs of higher education so that every student who starts college can finish with a degree. Imagine if families didn't have to struggle to send their kids to school, graduates could buy homes and start businesses without being held back by loans, and student-parents could afford quality childcare while pursuing their education.

That future is within our grasp. We can make it so cost is never a barrier for young people seeking to pursue a higher education. It's a simple but bold idea: Every student should be able to graduate from a public college or university in their state without taking on any student debt. That means earning a degree and being able to cover the full cost without taking out any loans—and for those students with family income below $125,000, it means paying absolutely no tuition at in-state public colleges and universities.

We call it the New College Compact. We'll make bold new federal investments in the form of grants to states that commit to meeting these goals. States will have to halt disinvestment in higher education, ramp up that investment over time, and work with public colleges and universities to cut costs, improve completion rates and learning outcomes, and do more to provide students from disadvantaged backgrounds with the tools they need to succeed.

Under the New College Compact, we will:

- **Eliminate college tuition for working families.** Students from families with incomes below $125,000 will pay no tuition at in-state public colleges and universities. That means more than 80 percent of American families will be able to send their kids to college without paying a dime.[45] And we will make community college tuition-free for all students.

---

45   "Selected Measures of Household Income Dispersion: 1967 to 2014," U.S. Census Bureau, P60-252, 2015, http://www2.census.gov/programs-surveys/demo/tables/p60/252/table4.pdf.

To help defray the costs of these initiatives, students will be expected to work ten hours a week. We will push to expand work opportunities that build career skills and introduce students of all backgrounds to public-service careers.

- **Create a dedicated $25 billion fund to provide support to private nonprofit schools, including historically black colleges and universities, working to improve affordability and student outcomes.** In addition to public colleges, many private nonprofit schools with modest endowments, including HBCUs, Hispanic-serving institutions, and other minority-serving institutions, help underserved students graduate and build the skills they need, including many first-generation college attendees. HBCUs graduate about half of all African American teachers in our country, large numbers of African American scientists and engineers, and nearly one in three African American college graduates with degrees in biology and math.[46] But too many HBCUs, HSIs, and other MSIs struggle to keep tuition affordable, and too many of their students are unable to complete their degrees. That's why our plan will create a dedicated fund to help these schools lower the cost of attendance and improve outcomes for students.

- **Promote college completion.** Less than half of all students who enter college graduate within four years. Too few low- and middle-income students are enrolling in the first place: over 80 percent of high-income high school graduates enroll in college, compared to around 60 percent of low- and middle-income

---

46 Marybeth Gasman and Thai-Huy Nguyen, "Historically Black Colleges and Universities (HBCUs): Leading Our Nation's Effort to Improve the Science, Technology, Engineering, and Mathematics (STEM) Pipeline." *Texas Education Review* 2 (1), 2014, 75–89; and "The Educational Effectiveness of Historically Black Colleges and Universities," U.S. Commission on Civil Rights, 2010, http://www.usccr.gov/pubs/HBCU_webversion2.pdf.

students.[47] Our plan will increase college enrollment by simplifying the federal student aid form families have to fill out, and providing early Pell notification and other key nudges to remove barriers and obstacles to applying to college in the first place. We will build on successful programs and make new grants to the colleges and universities that invest in student support, quality childcare, partnerships with early childhood providers, emergency financial aid, and other interventions proven to boost completion, especially for low-income and first-generation students.

- **Restore and protect Pell Grant funding.** We will restore year-round Pell Grant funding so that students have the support they need to take summer classes and meet their goal of completing college, and protect all Pell Grant funding so that low- and middle-income students who are not paying tuition under this plan also get the help they need to pay non-tuition expenses.

- **Expand educational pathways and reward innovation.** In addition to four-year and community college, many students are rebooting their careers and improving their economic prospects through innovative online programs as well as more traditional career and technical training programs. We will provide added support for rebooting careers and participating in lifelong learning in fields ranging from advanced manufacturing to healthcare services. We will also build on experiments allowing federal student aid to be used for programs with promising or proven records. We must ensure the integrity of online learning and will not tolerate programs that fall short.

---

47 "Table 326.10: Graduation Rate from First Institution Attended for First-Time, Full-Time Bachelor's Degree-Seeking Students at 4-Year Postsecondary Institutions," U.S. Department of Education, 2015; National Center for Education Statistics, https://nces.ed.gov/programs/digest/d15/tables/dt15_326.10.asp; and "Table 302.30: Percentage of Recent High School Completers Enrolled in 2-Year and 4-Year Colleges, by Income Level," U.S. Department of Education, 2015; National Center for Education Statistics, http://nces.ed.gov/programs/digest/d15/tables/dt15_302.30.asp.

Help young people break free from the crushing burden of student debt.

There are 40 million Americans with student debt, and too many of them struggle to keep up with loan payments.[48] Millions of borrowers are delinquent or in default. The collective amount of student debt is staggering: $1.2 trillion.[49] It has doubled since the onset of the financial crisis. It now exceeds debt from credit cards, car loans, and home equity lines of credit. And per-student debt levels have more than doubled in inflation-adjusted terms over the last two decades.

All of this debt is not just unfair to borrowers: It holds all of us back. It discourages borrowers from starting families and businesses and discourages others from enrolling in college. The parents and grandparents who have taken out or cosigned student loans have also suffered.

That's why we will:

- **Take immediate executive action to offer a three-month moratorium on student loan payments to all federal loan borrowers.** During this time-out from paying student loans, every borrower will be given the resources and targeted help they need to save money on their loans. With dedicated assistance from the Department of Education during this moratorium, borrowers will be able to consolidate their loans, sign up quickly and easily for income-based repayment plans, and take direct advantage of opportunities to reduce monthly interest payments and fees. Borrowers who are delinquent or in default will receive additional rehabilitation options to help them get back on their feet. We will also use the moratorium to crack down on for-profit colleges and loan servicers who have too often taken advantage of borrowers.

---

48 "Student Loan Borrowing and Repayment Trends, 2015," Federal Reserve Bank of New York, April 16, 2015, https://www.newyorkfed.org/medialibrary/media/newsevents/mediaadvisory/2015/Student-Loan-Press-Briefing-Presentation.pdf.
49 Nicholas Rayfield, "National student loan debt reaches a bonkers $1.2 trillion," *USA Today College,* April 8, 2015, http://college.usatoday.com/2015/04/08/national-student-loan-debt-reaches-a-bonkers-1-2-trillion/.

- **Reduce rates through refinancing.** Students should be able to refinance their loans at current rates, just as borrowers can refinance a car or home loan. The vast majority of federal borrowers will be eligible, as well as private borrowers who are current on their loans. Refinancing will help 25 million borrowers across the country, with the typical borrower saving $2,000 over the life of the loan.

- **Improve enrollment in income-based repayment.** Nobody should have to pay more than 10 percent of their monthly income on student loans, and college debt should be forgiven after twenty years—ten years if a borrower works in the public interest. We will simplify and expand enrollment in programs that follow these principles. We will also develop options for automatic enrollment.

- **Push employers to contribute to student-debt relief.** Employers must be part of the solution to the student-debt crisis. We will create a payroll-deduction portal for employers and employees that will simplify the repayment process. We will explore further options to encourage employers to help pay down student debt.

- **Help borrowers who are delinquent or in default.** Delinquent borrowers will receive additional help to enroll in income-based repayment to protect their credit, and borrowers in default will be given new rehabilitation and repayment options to help them get back on their feet.

- **Reward public service.** For Americans who engage in national service, we will dramatically expand AmeriCorps, double the award they receive for educational expenses, and make that award tax-free so those who engage in service can pay for college or pay down their debt. Teachers who teach in high-need areas or in subjects with teacher shortages, such as computer science or special education, will receive enhanced loan forgiveness.

Crack down on predatory schools, lenders, and bill collectors.

Too many students work hard and are supported by taxpayer dollars, only to emerge without a degree, or weighed down by excessive debt for a degree from a for-profit school that doesn't deliver what was promised. And when things go wrong and students default on their loans, it is students and taxpayers who end up holding the bag, not the colleges that took advantage of them in the first place. We need our nation's colleges to have strong incentives to keep debt low—and they should be penalized when their graduates are unable to repay their loans. We will embrace bipartisan efforts for schools to share in the risk of paying for college, and ensure that these efforts encourage, not discourage, enrollment in quality programs for underserved students.

- **Enact a new Borrower Bill of Rights.** This bill of rights will ensure accurate and timely advice on repayment options, including income-based modification for private borrowers who are in distress. We will also pursue a robust enforcement agenda to protect those rights. These standards will also be privately enforceable so that borrowers can assert their rights even when regulators fall short, which will further deter malfeasance by lenders and servicers.

- **Defend and strengthen the gainful employment rule.** We will set standards that ensure for-profit schools adequately support students to complete their degrees and prepare students for work.

- **Ban repeat offenders from contracts to service federal loans.** Servicers and bill collectors who consistently break the law and mislead or overcharge borrowers will no longer have access to contracts to service federal loans. We will also have zero tolerance for firms that overcharge servicemembers and veterans.

- **Protect borrowers from misleading, law-breaking for-profits.** We will crack down on law-breaking for-profits by expanding support for the Consumer Financial Protection Bureau, Federal Trade Commission, Department of Justice, and Department of Veterans Affairs to enforce laws against deceptive marketing, fraud, and other illegal practices. We will grant the Consumer Financial Protection Bureau the power to put into place strong consumer protections to ensure all borrowers understand all their options during the entire life cycle of a student loan and are not misled by either lenders or bill collectors.

- **Help defrauded students discharge debt.** In addition to pursuing every possible legal remedy against schools that defraud students, we will streamline the process by which students can cancel their debt so that it is not so cumbersome. We will also give defrauded GI Bill students another chance to use the education support they have earned.

Launch "Let's Start Something" to allow young entrepreneurs to defer their federal student loans while they get their ventures off the ground.

Thanks to the ingenuity of our entrepreneurs and the expertise of our workforce, America leads the world in driving growth and innovation. Developing new technologies and creating new industries translates ideas into more good-paying jobs right here in America. That's why, if we want to build an economy that works for everyone, not just those at the top, it's critical that we empower the next generation of entrepreneurs and innovators.

But today in America a smaller proportion of young people are starting new ventures compared to their predecessors. This is not for a lack of desire or ideas—surveys show that the millennial generation is aspiring, enterprising, and independent minded. But barriers like student debt and a lack of credit are holding young people back. Evidence shows that high student debt can pose a significant barrier to aspiring entrepreneurs and inhibit new business ventures.

It's time to take concrete action to remove the barriers that prevent so many young people from pursuing their dreams and empower them to start something—whether it's a social or civic enterprise, a small business, or a nonprofit. It's not enough to say we want more Americans to take the risks that make our country strong: We need to help them do it.

That's why we will:

- **Allow entrepreneurs to put their federal student loans on hold while they get new ventures off the ground.** For millions of young Americans, this will mean deferment from having to make payments on their student loans for up to three years—zero interest and zero principal—as they work through the critical start-up phase. We will also explore offering a similar loan deferment incentive not just to founders of enterprises but also to early joiners, such as the first ten or twenty employees.

- **Prioritize innovators that create jobs in distressed communities.** We will give innovators who decide to launch either new businesses that operate in distressed communities and create jobs and economic activity in those places, or social enterprises that provide measurable social impact and benefit, the opportunity to apply for forgiveness of up to $17,500 of their student loans after five years.

- **Invest in incubators and accelerators to help young people get their ventures off the ground.** Many of these programs are already operating in places across the country—through offering workspace, networks of mentors, access to investors, and other services. We will invest in a greater number of programs to expand this success.

Rewrite the rules so that more companies share profits with employees, and fewer ship profits and jobs overseas.

American workers are an asset to be invested in—not a cost to be cut. There are CEOs across the country that recognize that, and who are competing and winning in the global economy by creating good jobs and building their business rather than firing workers and stripping their companies for parts.

But too many businesses take the opposite view—which is bad for workers and bad for our country. Corporations that cut costs and fire workers in order to meet some arbitrary target on a quarterly report may reach their short-term goals, but they are hurting themselves in the long run. As we've noted, ours is a 70 percent consumption economy, which means that if we want strong, long-term economic growth, we need to raise incomes.[50] When workers' paychecks grow, America grows.

In 2014, thousands of employees at a grocery store chain in New England walked off the job—not to protest against their boss, but to save his job.[51] That's because Arthur T. Demoulas, one of the members of the family that runs Market Basket supermarkets, had been ousted from

---

50 "National Income and Product Accounts: Gross Domestic Product: First Quarter 2016," Bureau of Economic Analysis, BEA 16-32, 2016, http://www.bea.gov/newsreleases/national/gdp/2016/pdf/gdp1q16_3rd.pdf.
51 Tom Moroney, "America's Most Loved CEO Is Having the Best Comeback Ever." Bloomberg, July 31, 2015, http://www.bloomberg.com/news/articles/2015-07-31/market-basket-s-beloved-quirky-ceo-is-back-and-better-than-ever.

his position. Arthur T. was the champion of a generous profit-sharing program that gives all employees a stake in Market Basket's success—and puts extra money in their pockets, too. Eventually, the workers' walkout got the job done and Arthur T. was restored to his post—showing that investing in workers can pay off for executives, too.

We need to rewrite the rules in corporate America, bring a long-term view back to boardrooms and executive suites, and make sure that as our economy grows and our companies get more and more profitable, our workers get a piece of the pie.

That's why we will:

- Encourage companies to invest in their workers
- Support workers' rights and union rights
- Close the loopholes that help companies ship jobs and profits overseas
- Make trade a fair deal for American workers
- Stop Wall Street from ever wrecking Main Street again

Encourage companies to invest their in workers.

Every day, from the time he was a teenager until he retired
at age sixty-five, Hugh Rodham went to work at the Scranton Lace
Company. The machinery could be loud, and the work wasn't
always easy. But the men and women who worked there gave
their all to help build that company—and the company paid them
back in kind. From the early decades of the twentieth century,
the Scranton Lace Company didn't just offer health insurance,
they also had a profit-sharing plan—so when the company
was doing well, their employees would do well, too.
Hugh was my grandfather—and the work he did in Scranton helped
lay the foundation for who I am today.
—Hillary

Profit sharing is a win-win. The way it works is simple. When a company is doing well, workers get a portion of the company's profits, on top of a good base wage, just like executives commonly do. Profit sharing gives employees a stake in the outcome of their work, increases their take-home pay, and makes workers more satisfied with their job overall. So it makes sense that there's mounting evidence that profit sharing makes businesses more productive and innovative.

That's why we'll make it a national priority to get more companies to share profits with their employees and create a new tax credit for companies that do just that.

Employer-funded job training fell by more than 40 percent between 1996 and 2008, even as the premium on skilled workers has increased in a competitive global economy.[52] We need to encourage employers to invest in their workers again—because a well-trained, highly skilled workforce is key to our long-term prosperity as a nation.

---

52 "Economic Report of the President, Figure 3-27: Percent of Workers Receiving Employer-Sponsored or On-the-Job Training, 1996–2008," Council of Economic Advisers, 2015, https://www.whitehouse.gov/sites/default/files/docs/cea_2015_erp.pdf.

And we'll do more to support high-quality apprenticeship programs where you "earn while you learn," by creating a tax credit for businesses that hire apprentices from strong programs. Apprenticeships have been around for centuries because they work. In high-quality apprenticeship programs, like those run by many of America's major labor unions, workers of all ages learn real-world skills, spend time in the classroom working toward an advanced degree, and spend time on job sites, where they earn money for doing real-world work. While making college afford-able is essential to building an economy that works for everyone, not every good job of the future will require a four-year college degree. We are committed to supporting high-quality pathways for more Americans to learn and practice the trades and get jobs that provide dignity, a sense of purpose, and a middle-class salary.

Support workers' rights and union rights.

America's labor unions—from the ironworkers to the electrical workers, the pipe fitters to the carpenters, the teachers to the public employees, the laborers to the autoworkers—had a hand in literally building our economy. Along the way, they built the American middle class, by fighting for fairer wages, better benefits, and safer working conditions. Less than a century ago, it was the labor movement that successfully won the fight for a forty-hour workweek and an eight-hour work day.[53] And the labor movement fought alongside social justice activists and Democratic politicians to create our nation's bedrock social programs—from Social Security to Medicare to the Affordable Care Act.

But in recent decades, union membership has been on the decline, particularly in the private sector. That's bad news for all workers, whether they belong to a union or not. Overall union membership in the United States stands at 11 percent—a decline of nearly 10 percent from where it was in 2000.[54] During that same period, private-sector union membership declined by nearly 20 percent.[55] The middle class has shrunk and income inequality has increased in tandem with declining union membership, as fewer workers are able to enjoy the high-value training, benefits, and collective voice that come from being part of a union.

The United States has one of the lowest union membership rates in the world, more closely matching those of the Czech Republic and Mexico than other advanced industrial economies like Germany and Japan.[56] And low unionization rates make it harder for workers to stand up to their employers on issues like fair wages, workplace safety, sexual harassment, and wage theft.

That's why we will strengthen America's unions and stand up to governors and state legislatures that are trying to undermine workers' rights. Twenty six states have passed "right to work" laws, which make it

---

53   Louis Jacobson, "Does the 8-Hour Day and the 40-Hour Week Come from Henry Ford, or Labor Unions?" *Politifact*, September 9, 2015, http://www.politifact.com/truth-o-meter/statements/2015/sep/09/viral-image/does-8-hour-day-and-40-hour-come-henry-ford-or-lab/.
54   Calculation based on data from the U.S. Bureau of Labor Statistics.
55   Ibid.
56   "Trade Union Density," Organization for Economic Cooperation and Development (OECD), 2014, https://stats.oecd.org/Index.aspx?DataSetCode=UN_DEN.

harder for workers to organize and bargain collectively.[57] "Right to work" laws are wrong for workers and wrong for America. We need to make sure that no matter where you work, you can form or join a union if you want to and stand together with your colleagues to fight for better wages and fair scheduling. And we must be vigilant in cracking down on wage theft and making overtime count, so companies that pay well can't be undercut by competitors who force workers to accept poverty wages.

---

57   "Right to Work States: Do You Work in a Right to Work State?", National Right to Work Legal Defense Foundation, Inc., 2016, http://www.nrtw.org/rtws.htm.

Close the loopholes that help companies
ship jobs and profits overseas.

In Wisconsin, a company that was founded in 1885 as the maker of the first electric thermostat fell on hard times during the recession.[58] The financial problems at Detroit's Big Three automakers were sending shock waves down the supply chain. So Johnson Controls, which was by then a multinational company that makes car batteries and heating equipment, among other products, joined the automakers and other suppliers in lobbying Washington to pass legislation to save the American auto industry.

It's a good thing we did. Because the U.S. auto industry has come roaring back. The sector just had its best year ever. Without the auto rescue, not only would the Big Three have faltered, but countless smaller companies that make car parts and other goods would likely have closed their doors. We'd be telling a very different story about the industrial Midwest.

When Johnson Controls needed taxpayers to step in and help save the industry from which they derive so much business, Washington listened. But just a few years later, the company decided to pursue something called a "corporate inversion"—a tax game in which a company moves its headquarters overseas in name only, to skip out on paying their tax bill here in America.

Or take a company like Carrier, a major maker of air conditioners. Last year, United Technologies, Carrier's parent company, took home more than $7 billion in profits and more than $6.7 billion in federal contracts.[59] But shareholders pressured the company to boost profits even further. So one day in February, the 1,400 employees of a Carrier plant outside of Indianapolis were told their jobs were being shipped to Mexico.[60]

---

58 "Our History," Johnson Controls, 2016, http://www.johnsoncontrols.com/about-us/history.
59 United Technologies Corporation's operating profits for 2015 were $7,291 million. Source: "Financials: UTC Annual Report," United Technologies Corporation, 2015, http://2015ar.utc.com/assets/pdf/UTC_AR15_Financials .pdf. UTC received $6,793 million in federal contract funds in 2015. Source: "Contracts: All Recipients—FY 2015," USASpending.gov, 2015, https://www.usaspending.gov/Pages/TextView.aspx?data=FiscalYearMostFundedRecipients ByAwardType&AwardType=C&fiscalyear=2015.
60 Mark Abadi, "Watch 1,400 U.S. Workers Learn Their Jobs Are Moving to Mexico," *Business Insider,* February 12, 2016, http://www.businessinsider.com/carrier-workers-learn-jobs-are-moving-to-mexico-2016-2.

This kind of short-term thinking is bad for workers—and it's bad for business, too. Shipping jobs overseas may boost earnings in the short run, but in the long term, fewer consumers with money to spend means a weaker economy. Just as we need to reward companies that do the right thing by investing in their workers, we need to crack down on companies that turn their backs on America.

Make trade a fair deal for American workers.

Workers need more than tough talk on trade. They need a President who knows how to compete against the rest of the world and win for America.

Simply put, trade has not delivered for American workers the way it was supposed to. Too often, politicians have passed big trade deals that were good for corporations, but not for their workers—and only invested in our workers and communities here at home as an afterthought, if they've done it at all. There have been long-lasting downsides to some of the trade deals we have on the books. We've let too many communities be left out and left behind in the global economy. We've given companies tax break after tax break, only to have them pack up and move overseas anyway. We've encouraged corporations to think only about goosing their returns for the next quarter, not about making investments for the next quarter-century.

We know we can't just close our borders—we have only 5 percent of the world's population, and we need to sell things to the other 95 percent. Exports support more than 11 million jobs across the country, from big corporations to small businesses. Instead, we need to make sure that trade works for America.

Here's what we're going to do.

First, we're going to enforce the trade rules we have to the hilt to make sure American workers aren't being cheated. Too often, the federal government has put the burden of initiating trade cases on workers and unions, and failed to take action until after the damage is done and workers have been laid off.

That gets it exactly backward. The government should be enforcing the law from the beginning, and workers should be able to focus on doing their jobs. To make sure that gets done, we will establish and empower a new chief trade prosecutor reporting directly to the President, triple the number of trade enforcement officers who are responsible for cracking down on abuses, and build new early-warning systems so we can intervene before trade violations cost American jobs.

We will also hold other countries accountable for meeting internationally sanctioned labor standards—fighting against child and slave labor and for the basic rights of workers to organize around the world.

We're going to stand up to Chinese abuses. Right now, Washington is considering Beijing's request for "market economy" status. It sounds pretty obscure, but it's serious. If China gets market economy status, it will defang our anti-dumping laws, let cheap products flood into our markets, and undercut American workers. So we will reply with only one word: No.

With thousands of state-owned enterprises, massive subsidies for domestic industry, systematic, state-sponsored efforts to steal business secrets, and blatant refusal to play by the rules, China is far from a market economy. If China wants to be treated like a market economy, it needs to act like one.

And we need to do more to crack down on currency manipulation, which can be destructive for American workers. China, Japan, and other Asian economies kept their goods artificially cheap for years by holding down the value of their currencies.

Tough new surveillance, transparency, and monitoring regimes are part of the answer—but only part. We need to expand our toolbox to include effective new remedies, such as duties or tariffs and other measures.

Second, we're going to stop dead in its tracks any trade deal that hurts America. To earn our support, any trade deal must meet three tests: It must create good American jobs, raise wages here at home, and advance our national security. We believe the Trans-Pacific Partnership does not meet this high standard. We believe that it does not do enough to crack down on currency manipulation, which kills American jobs. We believe its "rules of origin" standard for what counts as a car that can get treaty benefits are too weak, giving Chinese-made auto parts a backdoor into U.S. markets. We worry that it puts the interests of drug companies ahead of patients and consumers. We have concerns about dispute settlement provisions that give special rights to corporations, but not to workers and NGOs. Therefore, we oppose the TPP—and that means before and after the election.

What's more, we need to review the trade agreements that we already have on the books, like NAFTA, and find ways to make them work for American workers, including by renegotiating them to better protect American jobs, international labor standards, and the environment.

Third, we can't look at trade policy in a vacuum: We need to make the kinds of investments at home that allow American workers and businesses to compete in the global economy. Years of Republican obstruction at home have weakened U.S. competitiveness and made it harder for Americans who lose jobs and pay because of trade to get back on their feet. Republicans have blocked the investments that we need and that President Obama has proposed in infrastructure, education, clean energy, and innovation. That's why we've made it a central priority to break through Washington gridlock to deliver major new investments in infrastructure, manufacturing, clean energy, and basic research—investments that will create good-paying jobs and make our economy more competitive for decades to come.

Fourth, we will fight for American exports. U.S. exports total more than $2 trillion, and exporters pay workers above-average wages. We will support the efforts of businesses large and small to tap new markets—both at home and internationally to support good-paying jobs and spur economic growth.

That is why we support the Export-Import Bank, which helps businesses reach new markets and compete for new customers. Nearly 90 percent of the Export-Import Bank's transactions directly support America's small businesses. And the Export-Import Bank levels the playing field for American businesses, ensuring that our companies never lose out on a sale to a foreign company because of attractive financing from other governments. Unfortunately, there are some in Congress who are fighting to shut down the bank—a step that would hurt American competitiveness and close new markets to our small businesses. We will stand for American workers by supporting the Export-Import Bank in the face of this misguided opposition.

We refuse to let anyone tell us we can't make things in America and sell them to the rest of the world. As our plan for revitalizing American manufacturing says, we can "make it in America"—and we will.

Stop Wall Street from ever wrecking
Main Street again.

The 2008 financial crisis saw reckless behavior on Wall Street send our economy into a tailspin. Nearly 5 million Americans lost their homes.[61] Nearly 9 million lost their jobs.[62] Some $18 trillion in household wealth was wiped out.[63]

It took hard work, but we got our economy growing again. And we put tough new rules on the books, including the Dodd-Frank Act, to protect consumers and curb recklessness and risk-taking on Wall Street. Those rules are working—which is a good thing.

Unfortunately, not everyone agrees. There are Republicans in Congress who are determined to go back to the bad old days where Wall Street could crash the economy, walk away without a scratch, and stick taxpayers with the bill for cleaning up the mess they caused. Republican members of Congress have tried to attach damaging deregulatory amendments to must-pass spending bills, and have called for rolling back commonsense efforts to prevent conflicts of interest by financial managers responsible for middle-class Americans' retirement savings. They have tried to hamstring the government's authority to regulate some of our riskiest financial institutions, and are committed to defunding and defanging the Consumer Financial Protection Bureau, an agency dedicated solely to protecting Americans from unfair and deceptive financial practices.

We can't afford to go backward. Making sure there is accountability on Wall Street is essential to building prosperity on every other street in America. That's why we have the toughest, most comprehensive plan to make sure Wall Street banks work for Main Street businesses and families.

---

61 Lisa Myers, Rich Gardella, and John W. Schoen, "No end in sight to foreclosure quagmire."
62 "Current Employment Statistics," U.S. Department of Labor, Bureau of Labor Statistics.
63 William Emmons and Bryan Noeth, "The Nation's Wealth Recovery Since 2009 Conceals Vastly Different Balance-Sheet Realities among America's Families," Federal Reserve Bank of St. Louis, 2013, https://www.stlouisfed.org/publications/in-the-balance/issue3-2013/the-nations-wealth-recovery-since-2009-conceals-vastly-different-balancesheet-realities-among-americas-families.

Our plan starts by pledging to veto any legislation that would weaken the protections enshrined in Dodd-Frank—and using the full force of that law to protect American consumers and businesses.

But we know the job of reforming our financial sector is not finished. We need to make sure no bank is too big to fail and no executive too powerful to jail. And we need tough, independent cops on the Wall Street beat to help get the job done.

That's why we will:

- **Require firms that are too large and too risky to be managed effectively to reorganize, downsize, or break apart.** The size and complexity of many financial institutions can create risks for our economy, both by making it more likely that firms will fail and increasing the severity of the economic damage failure would cause. That's why we will pursue legislation that enhances regulators' authority under Dodd-Frank to ensure that no financial institution is too large and too risky to manage. If firms can't demonstrate that they can be managed effectively, regulators have the explicit statutory authority to require that they reorganize, downsize, or break apart.

- **Impose a "risk fee" on the largest financial institutions.** To address the risk posed by size, leverage, and unstable short-term funding strategies, we will charge a graduated risk fee every year on banks with more than $50 billion in assets and other financial institutions that regulators believe merit stronger oversight. As firms get bigger and riskier, the risk fee they face will grow in size, discouraging large financial institutions from relying on excessive leverage and the kinds of "hot" short-term money that were particularly damaging during the crisis.

- **Strengthen oversight of the "shadow banking" system to reduce risk.** The so-called shadow banking sector—which includes certain activities of hedge funds, investment banks, and other non-bank financial companies—makes up more than a quarter of the global financial system and contributed significantly to the crash in 2008.[64] We believe we need more transparency of this sector, a better understanding of the risks it poses, and stronger tools to tackle those risks. Specifically, we will increase leverage and liquidity requirements for broker-dealers, impose strict margin requirements on the kinds of short-term borrowing that also played a major role in spurring the financial crisis, enhance public disclosure and regulatory reporting requirements, and strengthen the authority of the Financial Stability Oversight Council (FSOC) to address excessive risks.

- **Hold individuals, not just corporations, responsible when they break the law.** In America, no executive is too big to jail. We will enforce laws against the criminals who break them, plain and simple. That includes holding corporate officers and supervisors accountable when they knew about misconduct by their subordinates and failed to prevent it or stop it. We will extend the statute of limitations for major financial fraud, prohibit individuals in financial services convicted of egregious crimes from future employment in the industry, and make sure major corporate fines also cut into the bonuses of culpable executives, supervisors, and employees.

- **Ensure that prosecutors and regulators have the tools and resources they need to hold both individuals and corporations accountable for financial wrongdoing.** Right now, our efforts to investigate and prosecute financial crimes are under-resourced. We will increase funding for the DOJ, SEC, and CFTC so they have the resources and manpower they need to punish lawbreakers. And we will appoint tough, independent

---

64 "Shadow Banking: Strengthening Oversight and Regulation," Financial Stability Board, 2011, http://www.fsb .org/wp-content/uploads/r_111027a.pdf?page_moved=1.

regulators and ensure the Securities and Exchange Commission and the Commodity Futures Trading Commission are independently regulated. This is the only way we can ensure transparency and decrease conflicts of interest to make markets more stable and fair for everyone.

Ensure that Wall Street, corporations, and the super-wealthy pay their fair share.

Our tax code is rigged to favor corporations and multimillionaires and billionaires who can exploit loopholes and shelter income in order to avoid paying their fair share. There is essentially a "private tax system" for the wealthiest Americans that lets them lower their tax bill by billions, while working families play by the rules.

In 2013, the four hundred highest-income taxpayers—those making more than $250 million per year on average—paid an effective tax rate of just 23 percent, in part because of tax gaming and sheltering to reduce their tax bills.[65] Some multimillionaires can pay lower rates than their employees.[66] We believe that at a time when pay has risen far too slowly for working families, when America is underinvesting in our young people and our infrastructure, it is outrageous that the wealthiest can exploit loopholes and avoid paying their fair share.

---

65   "The 400 Individual Income Tax Returns Reporting the Largest Adjusted Gross Incomes Each Year, 1992–2013," U.S. Internal Revenue Service, 2015, https://www.irs.gov/pub/irs-soi/13intop400.pdf.
66   Thomas L. Hungerford, "An Analysis of the 'Buffett Rule,'" Congressional Research Service, R42043, 2012, http://www.fas.org/sgp/crs/misc/R42043.pdf.

That's why we will:

- Close tax loopholes and ensure the super-wealthy
  pay their fair share
- Ensure the wealthy, Wall Street, and big corporations pay their
  fair share—and provide families relief from rising costs
- Reform our business tax code to encourage
  long-term investment

Close tax loopholes and ensure the super-wealthy pay their fair share.

Too often, multimillionaires and billionaires play by one set of rules and working families play by another. By exploiting various loopholes in our tax code, the people who can afford to pay the most are able to get away with paying the least. That means middle-class families who play by the rules are left holding the bag.

Some patriotic billionaires like Warren Buffett are acknowledging the problem themselves. Buffett has pointed to his own taxes as proof of the fundamental unfairness of our system. He has earned billions and yet, year after year, he says he pays a lower effective tax rate than his secretary.[67]

Today, one-quarter of the top four hundred taxpayers who make on average $250 million per year pay less than a 20 percent effective federal income tax rate, and the top four hundred taxpayers pay an overall effective rate that is around 7 percentage points lower than the mid-1990s, a period of strong, shared economic growth.[68]

It's outrageous that multi-millionaires and billionaires are allowed to play by a different set of rules than hardworking families, especially when it comes to paying their fair share of taxes. We believe it's long past time to end this double standard.

We are committed to dismantling the private tax system that the ultra-wealthy have used to their benefit. This isn't about soaking the rich—it's simply about recognizing that no one makes a fortune in this country entirely on their own. No corporations could operate without publicly funded infrastructure helping them do so.

---

67 Warren E. Buffett, "Stop Coddling the Super-Rich," *New York Times,* August 14, 2011, http://www.nytimes.com/2011/08/15/opinion/stop-coddling-the-super-rich.html.
68 "The 400 Individual Income Tax Returns Reporting the Largest Adjusted Gross Incomes Each Year, 1992–2013," U.S. Internal Revenue Service.

That's why we will:

- **Ensure that hedge fund managers pay their fair share by closing the "carried interest loophole."** The "carried interest" loophole allows hedge fund, private equity, and other Wall Street money managers to avoid paying ordinary income rates on their earnings. With the top twenty-five hedge fund managers making more than every kindergarten teacher in the country combined, there is absolutely no justification for this tax loophole.

- **Implement the "Buffett Rule."** As a result of loopholes and the "private tax system" of lawyers and accountants who enable complex strategies to shelter and lower the bill on income for the most fortunate, some of the wealthiest taxpayers continue to pay low effective rates on their income. Named after Warren Buffett, the billionaire investor who has famously said it's wrong that some years he has paid a lower tax rate than his secretary, the "Buffett Rule" will ensure that every millionaire in America must pay at least a 30 percent effective tax rate. It's just basic fairness that the wealthiest Americans should not pay a lower effective tax rate than the middle class.

- **Impose a "Fair Share Surcharge" of 4 percent on multimillionaires.** The Buffett Rule is a good first step, but we will build on the foundation it would provide by implementing a 4 percent "Fair Share Surcharge" on multimillionaires. The surcharge would apply to incomes above $5 million per year—affecting only the top 0.02 percent of taxpayers in America. The experience of the past few years shows that a surcharge can directly raise the effective tax rates on the very-highest-income taxpayers in ways even their tax maneuvers cannot game.

As a result of President Obama securing the end of the high-income Bush tax cuts and other measures, the effective rate paid by the top four hundred taxpayers in America rose from less than 17 percent to 23 percent.[69]

- **Close the loophole that allows the super-rich to shelter their assets in retirement accounts.** Retirement savings are essential, but today about 1,000 taxpayers are gaming the system by accumulating close to $100 billion dollars in tax-preferred retirement accounts. These super-rich tax evaders are taking advantage of a system designed to help middle-class families save for retirement. We need to end this practice.

- **Restore fair taxation on multimillion-dollar estates.** Currently, some of the largest, multimillion-dollar estates in America are exempt from paying their fair share of taxes. By one estimate, wealthy estates have avoided more than $100 billion in estate taxes since 2000.[70] We will restore the estate tax to 2009 parameters, crack down on loopholes that let the ultra-rich disguise their assets, and lower the threshold at which the estate tax kicks in to $7 million for a couple, from its current high level of $11 million,[71] while protecting small family-owned businesses and family farms.

---

69   "Taxes," The White House, https://www.whitehouse.gov/issues/taxes.
70   Chye-Ching Huang and Brandon Debot, "Ten Facts You Should Know About the Federal Estate Tax," Center on Budget and Policy Priorities, 2015, http://www.cbpp.org/research/ten-facts-you-should-know-about-the-federal-estate-tax#_ftn8.
71   "Estate Tax Returns and Liability Under Current Law and Various Reform Proposals, 2011–2022," Tax Policy Center, T12-0318, 2012, http://www.taxpolicycenter.org/model-estimates/estate-tax-tables-2012/estate-tax-returns-and-liability-under-current-law-and.

Ensure the wealthy, Wall Street, and big corporations pay their fair share—and provide families relief from rising costs.

The measure of our economic success will be how much incomes rise for hardworking families and how many Americans can find good jobs that support a middle-class life with a sense of dignity and pride. That's what it means to have an economy that works for everyone, not just those at the top. That's the mission that has defined this campaign and should serve as our guiding principle moving forward. But in order to deliver progress, there are significant challenges we must first overcome.

Too many of our representatives in Washington are still in the grips of the failed theory of trickle-down economics. This flawed approach has been proven wrong repeatedly. But there are still people in Congress who insist on carving out tax breaks for the wealthy instead of investing in our future. And, too many special interests and too many lobbyists have stood in the way of progress while protecting the perks of the privileged few.

It's important to keep in mind that this is not just the case in Washington. Too many corporations have embraced policies that favor hedge funds and other big shareholders and top management at the expense of their workers, communities, and even their long-term value. At the same time, middle-class wages have stagnated, even as the basic costs of a middle-class life have grown.[72]

But slow wage growth is only part of the larger story of what happened to the American middle class. The other element is that middle-class Americans have been subject to unacceptable and rising costs just to meet basic needs. For instance, the cost of childcare has increased by nearly 25 percent during the past decade. And, new results from a Kaiser Family Foundation survey found that the average health insurance deductible this year is $1,318 for covering an individual—and has grown seven times faster than workers' wages since 2010.[73] That's not

---

72   Jennifer Erickson, ed., "The Middle Class Squeeze," Center for American Progress, September 2014, https://cdn.americanprogress.org/wp-content/uploads/2014/09/MiddeClassSqueeze.pdf.

73   "Employer Family Health Premiums Rise 4 Percent to $17,545 in 2015, Extending a Decade-Long Trend of Relatively Moderate Increases," press release, Kaiser Family Foundation, September 22, 2015, http://kff.org/health-costs/press-release/employer-family-health-premiums-rise-4-percent-to-17545-in-2015-extending-a-decade-long-trend-of-relatively-moderate-increases/.

to mention the concurrent rise in the cost of education, retirement, and housing. Moreover, for more than the past thirty years, there has been an increasing gap between how hard Americans work and how much they get paid. The Center for American Progress notes: "A worker today is almost 60 percent more productive than a worker in 1991 but has seen only half of that productivity growth translate into higher compensation."[74]

Every American willing to work hard should be able to find a job that pays enough to support a family. And in order to make that guarantee, we should be doing our part as well. That means making sure costs don't hold families back from achieving their goals and living up to their potential.

We will not raise taxes on the middle class. Instead, we'll close loopholes for the super-wealthy, Wall Street, and the largest corporations. And we will cut taxes to provide relief for the costs that middle class families face.

We have proposed specific tax relief for hardworking families so they can afford the basics of a middle-class life—from boosting paychecks to helping cope with the rising costs of health care and drugs, of raising children and caring for family members:

- **We will provide a tax credit to companies that share profits with their employees.** To help boost profits shared by working Americans, companies that share profits with their employees would receive a two-year tax credit equal to 15 percent of the profits they share—with a higher credit for small businesses. Shared profits eligible for the credit would be capped at 10 percent on top of employees' current wages. This would help companies overcome any initial costs of setting up a profit-sharing plan. After two years, companies that have established profit-sharing plans and enjoyed the benefits of them would no longer need the credit to sustain the plans.

---

74 Erickson, "The Middle Class Squeeze."

- **We will provide up to $5,000 in tax relief from excessive healthcare costs.** Americans struggling with excessive health costs that are not covered by their insurance will be eligible for a new refundable tax credit of up to $2,500 for an individual, or $5,000 for a family, to deal with substantial out-of-pocket healthcare costs. This refundable, progressive credit will help middle-class Americans who may not benefit as much from currently available deductions for medical expenses.

- **We will provide up to $1,200 in tax relief for caregiving.** We will offer a 20 percent tax credit to help family members offset up to $6,000 in caregiving costs for their elderly family members, allowing caregivers to claim up to $1,200 in tax relief each year. This will help defray the costs millions of American families face as more and more parents enter retirement.

Reform our business tax code to encourage long-term investment.

Our economy works best when businesses invest in America for the long term. We firmly believe businesses want a playing field that's both fairer and more competitive, in which the biggest multinational corporations no longer get undue special advantages over smaller, domestic businesses.

That's why we will:

- **Clamp down on corporate inversions.** In an inversion, businesses move their corporate residence abroad on paper in order to escape paying their fair share of taxes. Ending inversions and closing related loopholes will raise at least $80 billion[75] over the next decade. Congress should act immediately to prevent corporations from engaging in inversions. Without immediate action, inversions and related transactions will continue to erode our tax base. We need to reform and simplify our business tax code to encourage and reward investments in growth, innovation, and jobs here in the United States.

- **Limit the ability of multinationals to engage in "earnings stripping."** Multinational corporations use a practice called "earnings stripping" to shift profits from the United States to countries with lower tax rates, and to maximize high deductions in the United States. This loophole reduces the taxes they pay in the United States, putting them at an advantage over domestic and smaller competitors, and leaving others to pick up the burden. This is one of the main benefits of inversions and related transactions, making it easier to strip profits out of the United States. We will end the practice of earnings stripping to close a loophole that costs taxpayers as much as $60 billion over ten years.[76]

---

75 "Estimated Budget Effects of the Revenue Provisions Contained in the President's Fiscal Year 2016 Budget Proposal, Rep. (2015)," The Joint Committee on Taxation.
76 Ibid.

- **Close oil and gas loopholes and invest in clean energy.**
  Loopholes exist in the current federal tax code that act as "tax
  expenditures," meaning they provide taxpayer-funded subsidies
  to big oil and gas companies. Whether in the form of special ex-
  emptions, deductions, or credits, these loopholes are essentially
  direct government spending disguised as tax breaks. We have a
  plan to close these loopholes, and invest this spending instead
  in making America a clean-energy superpower by installing
  half a million solar panels by the end of our first term, and by
  generating enough renewable energy to power every home in
  America within ten years.

- **End the "Bermuda reinsurance" loophole.** This loophole
  allows firms that trade complex instruments like derivatives to
  game the system by exploiting provisions in foreign reinsurance law and sheltering their earnings in places like Bermuda
  to avoid paying taxes on their earnings. We will build on
  proposals from both President Obama and Republicans in
  Congress to finally close this loophole.

**Put families first and make sure
our policies match how you actually work
and live in the twenty-first century.**

If we want to build an economy that works for everyone, we need to put
our families first. That means matching our policies to how families
actually live in the the twenty-first century.

Families look a lot different today than they did thirty years ago.
The movement of women into the workforce has produced enormous
economic growth over the past few decades. Women are now the sole or
primary breadwinner in a growing number of households. But too many
people—men and women alike—are struggling to be good workers,
good parents, and good caregivers, all at the same time. They are trying
to manage the runaway costs of childcare and prescription drugs, worrying how they will care for an elderly or sick parent, and struggling to live
day to day on a paycheck that just won't budge.

We are asking families to rely on an old system of support in a new
economic reality. It's time for that to change. We will expand access to
affordable childcare and health care, guarantee paid family and medical
leave, and provide every American the confidence of a secure retirement.
And while we're at it—we're going to finally secure equal pay for women.
These are not luxuries—they are economic necessities. They are critical
to the future we want to build together.

That's why, together, we will:

- Fight for equal pay for women
- Ensure no family pays more than 10 percent
  of their income for childcare
- Guarantee paid family and medical leave
- Ease the financial burden for family caregivers
- Defend and enhance Social Security
- Expand health coverage and tackle mental health,
  addiction, and Alzheimer's disease

Fight for equal pay for women.

Women earn less than men across our economy, and women of color often lose out the most. All of this lost money adds up, and it means that women, on average, earn nearly $11,000 less per year than their male counterparts.[77] That's money that could be spent on rent or groceries, or put into a college fund. That's why fighting for equal pay is not only a women's issue, it's a family issue and an economic issue.

We need to address all the factors that leave women and their families with lower pay. That starts with giving women the legal tools to fight discrimination at work. But that's not enough. We must also address structural inequalities women face, including barriers that keep wages low in women-dominated professions and limit women's ability to enter high-paying fields like engineering and technology. That means promoting pay transparency across our economy to ensure women have the information they need to negotiate fairly. It means raising wages for the lowest-paid jobs in America, which are disproportionately held by women. And it means creating workplace policies like paid leave that allow parents to take care of their obligations at home without sacrificing pay at work.

Fighting for equal pay is critical to ensuring our economy works for everyone—including America's families. When a parent is short-changed on wages, an entire family is short-changed. And when families are short-changed, America is short-changed.

---

77 "The Wage Gap: The Who, How, Why, and What to Do," National Women's Law Center, April 1, 2016.

Women's earnings as a percentage of white men's earnings

Hispanic or Latina	55%
American Indian + Alaskan Native	59
African American	60
Native Hawaiian + Other Pacific Islander	62
White	75
Asian American	84

That's why we will:

- **Strengthen equal pay laws to combat discrimination.** In America, the average woman working full-time is paid 79 percent of what a man is paid. For African American women that number is 60 percent, and for Latinas it is 55 percent.[78] Based on this wage gap, a woman starting her career today will lose $430,480 over a forty-year career. An African American woman will lose $877,480—and a Latina will lose more than $1 million.[79] Discrimination—the fact that women are paid less than men for doing the same job—accounts for a significant portion of this wage gap. It's long past time to end wage discrimination. That starts with giving women the legal tools they need to fight discrimination at work by passing the Paycheck Fairness Act. The act will eliminate unfair legal defenses for pay discrimination, prohibit retaliation against an employee who discusses their own wages, and strengthen penalties for equal pay violations.

- **Promote pay transparency so that women have the information they need to negotiate fairly.** You can't stand up for equal pay if you don't know whether you are being paid equally. That's why we will promote pay transparency across our economy to ensure women have the information they need to negotiate fairly and fight for equal pay. Postings for new jobs or promotions should come with salary ranges; large companies should report on how fairly, or not, they're compensating workers, male or female; and we should recognize and reward those businesses and communities that are leading the way with best practices and real accountability. Pay transparency is our friend; the more women know, the more information they have to advocate for themselves and for each other.

---

78 "America's Women and the Wage Gap," National Partnership for Women and Families, 2016.
79 "The Lifetime Wage Gap, State by State," National Women's Law Center, April 4, 2016.

- **Raise the minimum wage, which is disproportionately earned by women.** The current federal minimum wage is too low to support a family. And because women represent nearly two-thirds of all minimum wage workers, many women are living that reality every day. [80] It's time to give American workers a raise. We support the workers fighting for a $15 minimum wage and the right to form or join a union in cities and states across the country. A higher federal minimum wage will help close the gender pay gap, lift millions of women out of poverty, and grow our economy by putting more money in families' pockets.

- **End the tipped minimum wage.** In most states, waitresses, bartenders, hairstylists, and others who rely on tips are paid even lower than minimum wage.[81] Some are paid as little as $2.13 per hour—and their tips are supposed to get them to at least a minimum wage. These workers are also more likely to face exploitation, wage theft, and sexual harassment. America is the only industrialized country in the world that requires tipped workers to take their income in tips instead of wages.
  It is time we end the "tipped minimum wage." Research has found that states with equal minimum wages for tipped workers have smaller wage gaps for women overall.[82]

- **Establish workplace policies that allow parents to take care of their obligations at home without sacrificing pay at work.** The high cost of childcare and lack of paid family and medical leave make it challenging for those with caregiving responsibilities—who are disproportionately women—to stay in and ultimately advance in the workforce. This time away from work means many women earn less over their careers, further contributing to the wage gap. Women who want to pursue a challenging and demanding career should be able to

---

80 "Minimum Wage," National Women's Law Center, last modified May 2015.
81 Ibid.
82 Ibid.

do so without worrying about how they're going to take care of their children or what will happen if a family member gets sick. That's why we will work to make high-quality childcare affordable for every American, provide tax relief to offset caregiving costs for elderly parents and grandparents, and finally guarantee paid family leave.

Guarantee no family pays more than 10 percent of their income for childcare.

In America, sending two children to a childcare center exceeds the average cost of rent.[83] And in the majority of states, it's more expensive to send an infant to a childcare center than a student to a four-year public college. That's outrageous.[84]

While families across America are stretched by skyrocketing costs, childcare has become more important than ever before—both as a critical work support for the changing structure of American families and as an essential component of a child's early development. These high costs severely squeeze working families, prevent too many children from getting a healthy start, and make it impossible for too many parents to stay in the workforce.

Stephanie from Chicago, Illinois, is one of these parents. Stephanie is a single working mother who makes too much to qualify for federal childcare assistance, but too little to afford high-quality care, which costs $700 a month in her neighborhood. So every day as she heads to work, she leaves her baby at an uncertified, overcrowded childcare provider that costs half as much as better care, but is less enriching—and possibly less safe—for her child.

We need to recognize that high-quality, affordable childcare is not a luxury—it's an economic necessity. That's why we will significantly increase our investment in federal childcare subsidies and provide tax relief to offset the cost of childcare for working families. We will also increase our investment in early learning programs and fight for policies like paid family leave, so that working parents can take time off to care for a new child. These policies will help us drive toward the critical goal of ensuring that no family pays more than 10 percent of their income for childcare. That is a commitment we will make to every family in America.

---

83   Michael Madowitz, Alex Rowell, Katie Hamm, "Calculating the Hidden Cost of Interrupting a Career for Child Care," Center for American Progress, June 21, 2016, https://www.americanprogress.org/issues/early-childhood/report/2016/06/21/139731/calculating-the-hidden-cost-of-interrupting-a-career-for-child-care/.
84   Elise Gould and Tanyell Cooke, "High Quality Child Care Is Out of Reach for Working Families," Economic Policy Institute, October 6, 2015, http://www.epi.org/publication/child-care-affordability/.

To guarantee that no family has to pay more than 10 percent of their income for childcare, we will:

- **Provide working parents paid time off to care for a new baby.** Parents are the first and best caregivers for their babies, yet a quarter of all women in America return to work less than two weeks after having a child, leaving them less time to bond with their newborns and increasing their risk of postpartum depression.[85] We will fight to pass twelve weeks of paid family leave, so mothers and fathers can care for their new babies, and parents can take time off work to care for an ill child without fearing for their jobs or paychecks.

- **Award scholarships of up to $1,500 per year to help as many as 1 million student-parents afford childcare.** Over 25 percent of all college students are balancing school with raising a child.[86] We will support them, not only because the economic benefit of a college degree lifts their own earnings prospects, but because it lifts the future earnings of their children too.[87] To support America's student-parents, we'll launch the Student-Parents in America Raising Kids (SPARK) program. SPARK will award scholarships of up to $1,500 per year to as many as 1 million student-parents to help defray the costs of childcare and other important expenses.

- **Increase access to childcare on college campuses by serving an additional 250,000 children.** Student-parents face many challenges, with greater financial and time constraints than many of their peers. College students who are parents leave school with an average debt that is 25 percent higher than non-parents'.[88] The demands of parenting mean student-

---

85 "Longer Maternity Leave Lowers Risk of Postpartum Depression," Press Release, University of Maryland Divi-sion of Research, December 12, 2013, http://www.umdrightnow.umd.edu/news/longer-maternity-leave-lowers-risk-postpartum-depression.
86 "4.8 Million College Students are Raising Children," Institute for Women's Policy Research, 2014.
87 "Benefits of Earning a College Degree," Education Corner.
88 Konrad Mugglestone, "Finding Time: Millennial Parents, Poverty, and Rising Costs," Lumina Foundation, 2015.

parents spend two hours less on average per day on educational activities.[89] And while nearly half of student-parents attend two-year colleges, less than half of all two-year college campuses in America offer on-campus childcare services.[90] Student-parents need our support. We will increase access to childcare on campus by boosting funding for campus-based childcare centers. We can serve an additional 250,000 children and improve the graduation and retention rates of student-parents.

- **Improve the quality of care by giving a RAISE to America's childcare workforce.** One of the key drivers of high-quality childcare is a supported and effective childcare workforce. Yet, despite the high cost of childcare, too many workers are not receiving a living wage, which fuels turnover and undermines the quality of care. To increase the quality of childcare in America and pay childcare workers for the true value of their worth, we will launch the Respect And Increased Salaries for Early Childhood Educators (RAISE) initiative. RAISE will fund and support states and local communities that work to increase the compensation of childcare providers and early educators, and provide equity with kindergarten teachers by investing in educational opportunities, career ladders, and professional salaries.

---

89   Ibid.
90   "Campus Child Care Declining Even As Growing Numbers of Parents Attend College," Institute for Women's Policy Research, 2014.

Guarantee paid family and medical leave.

No one should have to choose between keeping their job and taking care of a sick family member, and no woman should have to go back to work twenty-four hours after giving birth. But today the United States is the only developed nation in the world with no guaranteed paid leave of any kind.[91] In fact, only 13 percent of American workers have access to paid family leave through their employer[92]—with the lowest-paid workers up to four times less likely to have access to it than the highest-paid.[93]

In an economy where all parents in a household typically hold down a paying job, paid family and medical leave is core to our economic growth and competitiveness. Paid leave helps families remain economically stable, benefits children's early health and development by allowing parents to care for their newborn children, and reduces employee turnover. The availability of paid leave also bolsters our economy by enabling more Americans to participate fully in the workforce. To build an economy that works for everyone, we must ensure that we don't leave any talent on the sidelines.

That's why we will:

- **Guarantee up to twelve weeks of paid family and medical leave.** Working men and women should be guaranteed up to twelve weeks of paid family leave to care for a new child or a seriously ill family member, such as an ailing parent or a spouse with cancer. They should also be guaranteed up to twelve weeks of medical leave to recover from a serious illness or injury of their own.

- **Ensure at least a two-thirds wage replacement rate for workers.** To ensure families remain stable and supported

---

91 "The Economics of Paid and Unpaid Leave, Rep. (2014)," Council of Economic Advisers.
92 "Paid Leave," National Partnership for Women and Families, accessed July 2016, http://www.nationalpartnership.org/issues/work-family/paid-leave.html.
93 Heidi Shierholz, "Lack of Paid Leave Compounds Challenges for Low Wage Workers," U.S. Department of Labor blog, June 8, 2015.

during both joyful and stressful times, we will provide financial support to workers taking leave. Workers who have met a minimum number of hours the previous year should receive at least two-thirds of their current wages during leave so that low-income and middle-class workers receive the financial support they need. We can provide working families this support without imposing additional costs on businesses, including small businesses.

Ease the financial burden for family caregivers.

Nearly half of all Americans in their forties and fifties are part of the "sandwich generation," financially supporting both a child and an aging parent.[94] As baby boomers age, more and more families will face a similar struggle as they attempt to provide care for their loved ones—for elderly parents and grandparents, and for family members with disabilities or with serious or chronic illnesses.

Many of these families are forced to spend time out of the workforce, cut back on work hours, or use personal days to provide needed care to a loved one. Providing informal caregiving can strain family finances, with caregivers suffering lost wages, health insurance, and Social Security benefits. These families deserve our support.

That's why we will:

- **Provide tax relief to family members who care for ailing parents and grandparents.** Family caregivers often spend $5,000 or more in expenses related to their elders' care, but in many cases they receive no tax deduction or credit.[95] Caregiving can be a win-win for our families and our overall health system. This is why we will offer a 20 percent tax credit to help family members offset up to $6,000 in caregiving costs for their elderly family members, allowing caregivers to claim up to $1,200 in tax relief each year.

- **Expand Social Security by counting the hard work of caregivers and giving them the benefits they deserve.** Millions of men and women take time out of the paid workforce to raise a child, take care of an aging parent, or look after an ailing family member. Caregiving is hard work that benefits our entire economy. But when Americans take time off to take care of a relative, they don't earn credits toward Social Security retirement benefits.

---

94 Kim Parker and Eileen Patten, "The Sandwich Generation," Pew Research Center, January 30, 2013.
95 Amy Ziettlow, "Managing the Cost of Family Elder Care," Family Studies, November 20, 2014.

No one should face meager Social Security checks because they took on the vital role of caregiver for part of their career. Instead, Americans will receive credit toward their Social Security benefits when they are out of the paid workforce because they are acting as caregivers.

- **Build on the Caregiver Respite program.** Caring for a sick family member can exact a significant emotional and physical toll. Both caregiving family members and those they care for can benefit from occasional temporary relief. We will invest in programs to improve respite care access for family caregivers of children or adults of any age with support needs.

- **Launch a "Care Workers Initiative" to address the challenges faced by care workers.** Families also rely on home care workers to help them provide needed care to aging, disabled, or ill family members. Home care workers do hard, essential, compassionate work for millions of Americans. Despite the extraordinary care they provide, home care workers are often invisible and among the lowest paid of any occupation.[96] The low wages in these jobs lead to high turnover and limited training, creating care systems that do not work for the families depending on care or the workers who provide it. We will launch a "Care Workers Initiative" to create paths to professionalize the workforce through career ladders and apprenticeships; improve the rate-setting processes in the childcare and healthcare systems to ensure fair wages; provide care workers with an opportunity to come together and make their voices heard; and develop and enhance matching services to connect care workers with the families who need them.

---

96 "Occupational Employment and Wages," Bureau of Labor Statistics.

Defend and enhance Social Security.

Social Security is America at its best. Social Security reflects our shared belief that every American should be able to retire with dignity after decades of hard work. That no American should face poverty because he or she is disabled, or when a loved one dies. That we all have an obligation to each other. Social Security isn't just a program—it's a promise.

That's why we must defend against efforts to privatize or weaken Social Security, and enhance it to meet new realities. That starts with rejecting years of mythmaking claiming we cannot afford Social Security and that the only solution is to cut the benefits on which 90 percent of American seniors rely. Seniors have paid into these programs for a lifetime, and they've earned those benefits when they retire.

Rather than roll back Social Security, we will expand it for those who need it most and who are treated unfairly by the current system. We can make these critical enhancements, and preserve Social Security for decades to come, by asking the wealthiest to contribute their fair share.

The bottom line is this: We must defend and enhance Social Security to ensure the program continues to guarantee dignity in retirement for future generations.

That is why we will:

- **Oppose efforts to rob Americans of hard-earned benefits.**
  Social Security must remain what it has always been: a rock-solid benefit that seniors can always count on—not subject to the fluctuations of the stock market or to the budget whims of Congress. That's why we must fight back against any attempts to gamble seniors' retirement security on the stock market through privatization. We must oppose reducing annual cost-of-living adjustments. And we must stand firm against attempts to close Social Security's shortfall on the backs of the middle class. That means opposing reductions to annual cost-of-living adjustments. It means opposing efforts to raise the retirement age—an unfair idea that will particularly hurt the seniors who have worked the hardest throughout their lives. And it means opposing benefit cuts or tax increases that will impact that middle class.

- **Expand Social Security for those who need it most and who are treated unfairly by the current system—including women who are widows.** The poverty rate for widowed women sixty-five or older is nearly 90 percent higher than for other seniors, in part because when a spouse dies families can face a steep benefit cut. For a two-earner couple, those benefit cuts can be as much as 50 percent. We have to change that by reducing how much Social Security benefits drop when a spouse passes away. The loss of a spouse is hard enough and should not be compounded by the added burden of financial hardship or the threat of poverty. In fact, data shows that women rely on Social Security most of all.

- **Support, rather than punish, those who take time out of the workforce to care for a child or sick family member.** Millions of Americans take time out of the paid workforce to raise a child, take care of an aging parent, or look after an ailing family member. Caregiving is hard, admirable work that benefits our entire economy. Paid family leave will help us in the fight to protect caregivers at the outset, and we will push for it from the beginning of the next administration. However, it can be easy to forget that when Americans take time off to care for relatives, they often face reductions in their long-term Social Security benefits. No one should face meager Social Security checks because they took on the vital role of caregiver.

- **Preserve Social Security for decades to come by asking the wealthiest to contribute more.** Social Security must continue to guarantee dignity in retirement for future generations. There is no way to accomplish that goal without asking the highest-income Americans to pay more, so the middle class doesn't have to foot the bill, including options to tax some of their income above the current Social Security cap, and taxing some of their income not currently taken into account by the Social Security system.

Expand health coverage and tackle mental health, addiction, and Alzheimer's disease.

Quality, affordable health care is not a luxury—it should be a right for every American. We are closer than ever before to making affordable health care a reality for all American families. The Affordable Care Act has translated into real change in people's lives—and we need to keep building on it. Twenty million Americans have gained coverage. Millions of young people are able to stay on their parents' plans. Insurance companies can no longer discriminate against people with preexisting conditions or charge women higher rates just because of their gender.[97]

But across America, many families are struggling under the weight of healthcare costs. Out-of-pocket expenses are growing faster than wages, forcing families to put their hard-earned pay toward deductibles, copays, and coinsurance for medical expenses. For too many, these costs have put health coverage entirely out of reach.

Too many are still struggling to afford the high cost of prescription drugs. Every month, 90 percent of seniors and around half of all Amer-

---

97 "Key Facts and Reports: The Fifth Anniversary of the Affordable Care Act," press release, The White House, March 22, 2015.

icans take a prescription drug—and too often, the costs are crippling.[98] A typical senior on Medicare spends over $500 per year to pay for prescription drugs, and individuals with chronic health conditions or serious illnesses can spend thousands of dollars more.

And there are health issues affecting tens of millions of Americans that our current system is ill-equipped to handle. More than 5 million Americans suffer from Alzheimer's disease, a number that is expected to grow threefold to nearly 15 million by 2050—but we have no way to prevent, effectively treat, or cure this devastating illness.[99] Tens of millions of Americans, including a large number of veterans, struggle with mental health issues. But too many insurers do not adequately cover mental health treatment, and our society stigmatizes those with mental illness and treats mental health less seriously than physical health. Nearly 23 million Americans struggle with drug or alcohol addiction, but only a small fraction get treatment, and too many land in prison.

We will:

- Defend and enhance the Affordable Care Act to slow the growth of out-of-pocket costs and expand coverage—including offering a public-option choice, and investing in community health centers
- Crack down on rising prescription drug costs and hold pharmaceutical companies accountable
- Prevent, effectively treat, and make an Alzheimer's cure possible by 2025
- Put treatment of mental health on par with that of physical health, and end the stigma associated with treatment
- Combat America's deadly epidemic of drug and alcohol addiction

---

98 Topher Spiro, Maura Calsyn, and Thomas Huelskoetter, "Enough is Enough," Center for American Progress, September 18, 2015, https://www.americanprogress.org/issues/healthcare/report/2015/09/18/121153/enough-is-enough/.
99 "2016 Alzheimer's Disease Facts and Figures," Alzheimer's Association, https://www.alz.org/documents_custom/2016-facts-and-figures.pdf.

Defend and enhance the Affordable Care Act to slow the growth of out-of-pocket costs and expand coverage.

The Affordable Care Act was the single-biggest expansion of healthcare coverage since the creation of Medicare and Medicaid in 1965. About 20 million more Americans receive coverage today because of the Affordable Care Act, and, contrary to the doomsday predictions of its opponents, the law is already helping to slow the growth of healthcare costs.

Sarah is one of the millions whose life was changed by the Affordable Care Act. Ten years ago, she learned she had multiple sclerosis. Without the Affordable Care Act, she would have come up against a lifetime cap on benefits and been denied a new policy, leaving her in financial jeopardy. Sarah says the Affordable Care Act allowed her to finally be self-sufficient and restored her peace of mind.

These are real accomplishments we should be proud of, but our work is far from finished. We must continue our fight to bring down healthcare costs and at last achieve universal health coverage.

To expand coverage for millions of Americans and finally put universal health care within reach, we will:

- **Encourage all states to expand Medicaid with new incentives.** Despite national coverage gains, the refusal of many governors and legislatures to expand Medicaid has kept millions of working families uninsured. Roughly 4 million Americans are now in a "coverage gap"—not eligible for a subsidy on a health insurance exchange but also not eligible for Medicaid because their state has refused to take advantage of the Affordable Care Act's Medicaid expansion.[100] If we don't expand Medicaid, too many Americans will be left uninsured. That's why we must continue to incentivize states to do right by their residents by offering any state that signs up for Medicaid expansion a 100 percent match for the first three years.

---

100 "Fact Sheet: Health Care Accomplishments," Press Release, The White House, March 22, 2016.

- **Invest in navigators, advertising, and other outreach activities to make enrollment easier.** Today, as many as 16 million people or half of all those uninsured are eligible for but not enrolled in virtually free Medicaid coverage or exchange coverage for as little as $100 a month or less.[101] We must ensure that anyone who wants to enroll can understand their options and enroll by dedicating more funding for outreach and enrollment efforts.

- **Expand access to affordable health care to families regardless of immigration status.** All families deserve access to health care—that includes America's immigrant families too. We will allow any family, regardless of immigration status, to buy into the Affordable Care Act exchanges. Families who want to purchase health insurance should be able to do so.

- **Support a public option to broaden choices—and let people over fifty-five buy into Medicare.** We will pursue efforts to give Americans in every state the choice of a public-option insurance plan, and to expand Medicare by allowing people fifty-five years or older to opt in while protecting the traditional Medicare program.

- **Significantly expand investments in community health centers to broaden access to primary care.** One critical component of establishing universal primary care is to expand our proven system of Federally Qualified Health Centers. Today, 25 million people in the United States get their care from these community health centers each year. We must significantly expand that coverage so that every American, regardless of where they live, has good-quality primary health care available to them at a cost they can afford. We are committed to doubling the funding for primary care services at community health

---

101   "New Estimates of Eligibility for ACA Coverage among the Uninsured," The Henry J. Kaiser Family Foundation, January 22, 2016, http://kff.org/health-reform/issue-brief/new-estimates-of-eligibility-for-aca-coverage-among-the-uninsured/.

centers over the next decade. In doing so, we will dramatically expand access to millions more people. This means extending the current mandatory funding under the Affordable Care Act and expanding it by $40 billion over the next ten years. And we support President Obama's call for a near tripling of the size of the National Health Service Corps.

To slow the growth of out-of-pocket healthcare costs, we will:

- **Require health insurance plans to provide three sick visits without counting toward deductibles every year.** The Affordable Care Act required nearly all plans to offer many preventive services, such as blood pressure screening and vaccines, with no cost sharing at all. But because average deductibles have more than doubled over the past decade, many Americans still have to pay a significant cost out-of-pocket toward their deductible when they get sick and need to see a doctor. We need to build on the Affordable Care Act and require insurers and employers to provide up to three sick visits to a doctor per year without needing to meet the plan's deductible first. No one should have to worry about paying large out-of-pocket costs when they get sick and need a checkup during the year, whether it's for a common cold or a more harmful illness. A person with private coverage could save over $100 per year.[102]

- **Provide a new progressive, refundable tax credit of up to $5,000 per family for excessive out-of-pocket costs.** For families that struggle with out-of-pocket costs even after free primary care visits, we will provide progressive, targeted new relief. Americans with health coverage will be eligible for a new refundable tax credit of up to $2,500 for an individual, or $5,000 for a family, to deal with substantial out-of-pocket healthcare costs.

---

102 "Primary Care Visits Available to Most Uninsured but at a High Price," Johns Hopkins Bloomberg School of Public Health, May 5, 2015, http://www.jhsph.edu/news/news-releases/2015/primary-care-visits-available-to-most-uninsured-but-at-a-high-price.html.

This refundable, progressive credit will help middle-class Americans who may not benefit as much from currently available deductions for medical expenses.

- **Strengthen authority to block or modify unreasonable health insurance rate increases.** States should have the power to prevent insurance companies from imposing excessive, double-digit premium rate increases without a clear justification. But unfortunately, not all states have that authority. That's why we will create a fallback process for states that do not have the power to modify or block health insurance premium rate increases. This will help keep premiums lower for Americans.

- **Vigorously enforce anti-trust laws to scrutinize mergers and ensure they do not harm consumers.** For several years, consolidation and mergers have risen in the health industry—both on the provider side and on the insurer side. Mergers should be beneficial for consumers. That's why we will ensure America's anti-trust authorities have the resources and vigor to monitor the changing industry landscape and to move quickly to investigate mergers or business practices that could harm consumers.

- **Build on delivery system reforms that reward value and quality.** In order to keep costs down and improve quality, we must demand that our healthcare system provide value to every American. That means we need to continue to shift away from the "fee for service" payment system that rewards providers who prescribe excessive tests and unnecessary procedures, driving up costs without quality. And it means we need to aggressively root out fraud and abuse that hurts Americans and adds to taxpayer costs.

- **The healthcare system needs to reward value-driven care.** This will help to ensure providers offer the best possible care at the highest value to patients—rather than letting costs rise higher and higher without more effective care. That's why we must expand value-based delivery system reform in Medicare and Medicaid, and pursue public-private efforts that incentivize employers and insurers to expand these proven payment models so every American can benefit.

- **Encourage the next generation of health innovation and entrepreneurship.** Entrepreneurs are at the cutting edge of our health system, letting Americans monitor their heart rhythms, matching patients with doctors, making prices more transparent and easier to understand, and even offering new ways of providing health insurance coverage that are accessible and affordable. We will expand access to high-quality data on cost, care quality, and health delivery system performance while ensuring there are careful protections for privacy and security. This will empower entrepreneurs to build new products and services, while helping patients and doctors make informed healthcare choices.

Crack down on rising prescription drug costs and hold pharmaceutical companies accountable.

Too many American families and seniors are being squeezed by rising drug costs. At the same time, the largest pharmaceutical companies are together earning $80–$90 billion per year in profits at higher margins than other industries.[103] They're receiving billions of dollars in taxpayer support for basic research, but spending more on marketing than research and development. And they're charging Americans thousands of dollars for new drugs—often at much higher costs than in other developed nations.

At a town hall in New Hampshire, one man who knows this challenge all too well shared his story. He has been HIV-positive for more than twenty-five years. To stay healthy, he takes one drug every day. It costs $2,600 a month. His insurance used to cover it, but when his employer switched insurance providers, he had to go without his medicine for an entire week because he couldn't afford it on his own. Extreme costs like this should never prevent people from getting the critical treatment they need.

To lower prescription drug costs, we must hold pharmaceutical companies accountable by stopping excessive profiteering and marketing. And we must implement policies that directly relieve the cost pressures American families face when buying prescription drugs.

That's why we will:

- **Stop direct-to-consumer drug company advertising subsidies, and reinvest funds in research.** Almost every country in the industrialized world bans or severely restricts direct-to-consumer advertising for prescription drugs because it increases drug costs, and can include confusing, misleading, or incomplete information if not regulated effectively. In America,

---

103 Corrine Jurney, "2016 Global 2000: The World's Largest Drug and Biotech Companies," *Forbes*, May 27, 2016, http://www.forbes.com/sites/corinnejurney/2016/05/27/2016-global-2000-the-worlds-largest-drug-and-biotech-companies/#3775e3e1d50c.

the tax code subsidizes and encourages it. It's time to eliminate drug company write-offs for direct-to-consumer advertising. This will save the government billions of dollars over the next decade—money we will invest in research by making the research and development tax credit permanent.

- **Require drug companies that benefit from taxpayers' support to invest in research, not marketing or profits.** Americans should get the value they deserve for the billions of dollars in support they provide through federal investment in basic research and incentives for research and development. Drug companies should not be allowed to reap excessive profits or spend unreasonable amounts on marketing if they want to receive support that is designed to encourage lifesaving and health-improving treatments. Pharmaceutical companies that benefit from federal support should be required to invest a sufficient amount of their revenue in research and development. If they do not meet targets, we will require they boost their investment or pay rebates to support basic research.

- **Cap monthly and annual out-of-pocket costs for prescription drugs.** Americans should be able to afford prescriptions for their conditions throughout the year, and not have to stop taking a needed medication. Following the example of states like California and Maine, we will require health insurance plans to place a monthly limit of $250 on covered out-of-pocket prescription drug costs for individuals. This will provide desperately needed financial relief to patients with chronic or serious health conditions and benefit up to one million Americans a year.

- **Allow Americans to import drugs from abroad—with careful protections for safety and quality.** It is fundamentally unfair that drug companies charge far lower prices abroad for the same treatment while imposing higher prices on Americans. Countries in Europe often pay half of what Americans pay for the same drugs. We will allow Americans to safely and securely import drugs for personal use from foreign nations whose safety standards are as strong as those in the United States.

•   **Allow Medicare to negotiate drug and biologic prices.** Medicare should use its leverage with more than 55 million enrollees to negotiate and drive down drug and biologic prices for seniors and others in the program.[104] Today, drug prices in Medicare are negotiated by a disparate set of benefit managers instead of using the full bargaining power of the program. We will drive the best bargain for Americans, and especially for senior citizens, by allowing Medicare to negotiate drug prices, notably for high-cost drugs with limited competition.

---

104   "On its 50th anniversary, more than 55 million Americans covered by Medicare," Press Release, Centers for Medicare & Medicaid Services, July 28, 2015.

Prevent, effectively treat, and make an Alzheimer's cure possible by 2025.

Alzheimer's disease now ranks as the sixth-leading cause of death in the United States and is the only cause in the top ten for which we lack the ability to prevent, cure, or even slow the progress of the disease.[105] In addition to those who directly suffer from the disease, Alzheimer's takes a toll on the millions of family members who care for their loved ones. Too often, these quiet caregivers are forced to choose between their work and taking care of an ailing parent.

Not only does Alzheimer's carry devastating human costs, it also poses a significant financial hardship on families and our economy. Alzheimer's is also one of the costliest diseases in America. Its annual cost, combined with those of related dementias, exceeds $230 billion. Recent reports suggest that by 2050 the total cost for Alzheimer's may exceed $1 trillion per year.[106]

Keith is a public school librarian whose mother is one of the millions of Americans suffering from Alzheimer's. She is eighty-four and Keith takes care of her, but he can't afford to hire a caregiver for her during the day. So instead, he brings her to work with him. Millions of families across the country face hard choices like Keith's—and for many of them, they don't have even the limited flexibility that he does to balance work and caregiving.

In its human and financial costs, Alzheimer's stands out—yet the fight against Alzheimer's and other dementias is underfunded relative to the tremendous toll the disease takes. As a result, while researchers have begun to illuminate the basis of this dreaded disease, our progress is far too slow.

In the grand tradition of American scientific discovery, we will take what was once a remote possibility—developing a cure for Alzheimer's—and organize a broad national effort to tackle the disease. It will require that we invest needed resources, engage and inspire leaders across sectors, and develop effective interventions to prevent and

---

105 "Changing the Trajectory of Alzheimer's Disease: How a Treatment by 2025 Saves Lives and Dollars," Alzheimer's Association, 2015, https://www.alz.org/documents_custom/trajectory.pdf.
106 Ibid.

effectively treat Alzheimer's and related dementias, thereby making a cure possible. This will be a critical milestone on the pathway to a cure, potentially saving millions of lives and billions of dollars—and it is within our grasp.

To prevent, effectively treat, and make an Alzheimer's cure possible by 2025, we will:

- **Dedicate a historic decade-long investment of $2 billion per year for Alzheimer's research and related disorders.** Leading researchers have determined an annual investment of $2 billion is needed to prevent and effectively treat Alzheimer's and make a cure possible by 2025.[107] Making this bold new research investment in preventing and effectively treating Alzheimer's will pay off not just for Alzheimer's disease but for a range of neurodegenerative illnesses, such as Parkinson's disease, Lewy body dementia, and frontotemporal dementia. It will also help us understand the intersection of Alzheimer's with other conditions, including the high rate of individuals with Down syndrome who experience early-onset Alzheimer's.

- **Ensure a reliable stream of funding between now and 2025.** Just as important as increasing the level of investment, we must fight to make funding predictable and reliable between now and 2025 so that researchers can work consistently toward effective treatments and a cure. This gives researchers greater freedom to pursue the big, creative bets—including cross-collaboration with researchers in related fields—that can result in dramatic payoffs not only for Alzheimer's but for other neurodegenerative illnesses as well.

---

107   Ibid.

- **Establish a plan of action with NIH, leading researchers, and other stakeholders to see the 2025 goal through.** We will appoint a top-flight team to oversee this initiative and consult regularly with researchers to ensure progress toward achieving the treatment target. Reaching the goal will require investments across the drug development cycle, from basic research, to applied and translational research, to public-private partnerships for clinical research, and working to recruit participants for clinical trials.

- **Ease the burden of Alzheimer's for caregivers.** While we fight to make a cure possible by 2025, we must also do more to support family members who do the difficult work of caring for their loved ones. We will provide tax relief to family members who care for ailing parents and grandparents, count the hard work of family caregivers toward Social Security, expand access to family caregiver respite, and support paid family leave for caregivers.

**Put treatment of mental health on par with that of physical health,
and end the stigma associated with treatment.**

One-fifth of all adults in the United States—more than 40 million
people—are coping with a mental health problem, and close to 14
million live with a serious mental illness such as schizophrenia or bi-
polar disorder.[108] Moreover, many of these individuals have additional
complicating life circumstances, such as drug or alcohol addiction,
homelessness, or intersection with the criminal justice system. Veterans
in particular are disproportionately impacted, with close to 20 percent
of those returning from the wars in Iraq and Afghanistan experiencing
post-traumatic stress or depression.[109] The problem is not limited to
adults: An estimated 17 million children in the United States experience mental health problems.

These Americans and their families need our support. The economic
impact of mental illness on our country is enormous—nearly $200
billion every year just in lost earnings—but the human cost is worse.[110]
Too many Americans are being left to face mental health problems on
their own, and too many individuals are dying prematurely from associated health conditions that could have been treated. We must do better.
Taking on this challenge will require a thorough and serious approach.
The next generation must grow up always knowing that mental health
is a key component of overall health and there is no shame, stigma, or
barriers to seeking care.

Rachel, a young woman living in Miami, has suffered from depression
since she was a child. But until 2014, when she enrolled in an Affordable
Care Act plan that covered mental health care, she had never been able to
see a doctor and get help. Instead of taking her own life, she has now turned
her life around. No one should be denied mental health care because they
cannot afford it or because their insurance does not cover treatment.

---

108   National Alliance on Mental Illness.
109   "One in Five Iraq and Afghanistan Veterans Suffer from PTSD or Major Depression," Press Release, RAND
Corporation, April 17, 2008, http://www.rand.org/news/press/2008/04/17.html.
110   "Mental Disorders Cost Society Billions in Unearned Income," Press Release, National Institute of Mental
Health, May 7, 2008, http://www.nimh.nih.gov/news/science-news/2008/mental-disorders-cost-society-billions-in-
unearned-income.shtml.

That's why we will:

- **Promote early diagnosis and intervention.** The majority of American adults living with lifelong mental illnesses show signs of distress at an early age. Yet, two-thirds of children with mental health problems do not receive treatment at all, and children in high-risk groups—those in juvenile justice settings, in the child-welfare system, or who are the children of mothers who experienced depression during or after pregnancy—are particularly underserved.[111] We will increase public awareness of mental health, scale up efforts to help pediatric practices and schools support children facing these problems, help providers share best practices, and ensure that college students have access to mental health services.

- **Launch a national initiative for suicide prevention.** More than 40,000 Americans take their own lives every year, making suicide the tenth-leading cause of death nationally.[112] We will create a national initiative around suicide prevention that is headed by the Surgeon General that places mental health programs in high schools and colleges.

- **Integrate our nation's mental and physical healthcare systems, so that healthcare delivery focuses on the "whole person."** There are more people who need mental health services than there are resources to provide them. We will foster integration so that treatment for mental health is available in more general healthcare settings. We will also support the creation of high-quality, integrated community health centers in every state.

---

111 "Majority of Youth with Mental Disorders May Not Be Receiving Sufficient Services," National Institute of Mental Health, January 4, 2011.
112 "National Center for Health Statistics: Suicide and Self-inflicted Injury," Centers for Disease Control and Prevention, February 2016.

- **Enforce mental health parity to the full extent of the law.** A patient seeking mental health services is twice as likely to be denied coverage by a private insurer as a patient seeking general medical care.[113] We will work to fully enforce mental health parity laws by launching randomized audits to detect parity violations, enforcing disclosure requirements so insurers cannot conceal practices of denying care, and creating a process for patients to report parity violations when they occur.

- **Improve access to housing and job opportunities.** We must ensure that individuals with mental health issues have access to a full range of housing and employment supports so they can lead independent and productive lives. To do that, we will expand community-based housing opportunities and work with private employers and state and local mental health authorities to share best practices around hiring and retaining individuals with mental health conditions.

---

113   "Long Road Ahead: Achieving True Parity in Mental Health and Substance Use Care," National Alliance on Mental Illness, 2015.

Combat America's deadly epidemic of drug and alcohol addiction.

From our biggest cities to our smallest towns, and from our richest enclaves to our poorest neighborhoods, substance use disorders touch millions of American families. This is not a problem that appeared overnight. But it is one that is getting worse, and the costs of not addressing this crisis are too high to ignore, from overloaded healthcare and criminal justice systems to hundreds of thousands of lives lost. While nearly 23 million Americans suffer from a substance use disorder, only about one in ten receive treatment.[114] That must change.

This is a crisis that affects those suffering from addiction and their loved ones alike. Pam is a grandmother living in New Hampshire whose daughter is addicted to heroin. Pam's daughter is in and out of treatment and often on the streets, and Pam and her husband are raising their grandson, because their daughter simply cannot care for him.

In West Virginia—where more people per capita die from opioid and heroin overdoses than any other state—a bright young woman named Chelsea survived unlikely odds. She started using drugs when she was only twelve years old, after meeting a friend on the playground who brought her to her first party. Her life began to spiral, from dating her drug dealer to stealing money from her parents. Eventually she was caught with drugs and sentenced to prison time. She made a commitment to turn her life around. Chelsea is thankful to be in recovery, but she has also had to bury too many friends. She is working toward a master's degree in social work to try and help other young people like her.

This quiet epidemic demands that we work together to keep our families healthy and safe. That's why we will launch a new partnership between the federal government, states, and local communities to prevent and treat addiction. The idea is simple: States will be eligible for generous new grant funding if they work with local stakeholders to put forward a comprehensive plan that addresses key priority areas, including prevention, treatment and recovery, emergency response, prescribing

---

114 "DrugFacts: Treatment Statistics," National Institute on Drug Abuse, March 2011.

practices, and criminal justice reform. And while states develop and implement plans to address these issues in their communities, we must take concrete federal action to combat drug and alcohol addiction across America.

Through federal-state partnerships to prevent and treat addiction, we will:

- **Ensure that every person suffering from drug or alcohol addiction can access the comprehensive, ongoing treatment he or she needs and stay in recovery.** Substance use disorders are chronic diseases that affect the brain. Like chronic diseases that affect other systems of the body, they cannot be overcome with one-off interventions. Recovery is only possible through effective and ongoing care, not neglect or stigmatization or episodic treatment.

- **Put naloxone in every first responder's medical kit.** Naloxone, a rescue drug that stops opioid overdoses from becoming fatal, must be in the basic toolkit of every first responder. That's why we will support states that create naloxone training programs for first responders, and we will support states that help local police departments, fire departments, and EMTs purchase naloxone.

- **Give prescribers the information and training they need to treat patients with chronic pain.** About eighty Americans die every day from opioid abuse.[115] To prevent new cases, we must ensure that prescribers have the information and training they need to treat patients with chronic pain appropriately, and to identify patients who may be at risk of, or already experiencing, addiction. We will support states that require licensed prescribers to have a minimum amount of training, as well as

---

115 "Injury Prevention and Control: Opioid Overdose," Centers for Disease Control and Prevention, 2016.

those that require prescribers to consult a prescription drug monitoring program before writing a prescription for controlled medications.

- **Prioritize rehabilitation and treatment over prison for low-level and nonviolent drug offenses.** Sixty-five percent of people in prisons and jails meet medical criteria for substance use disorders, yet most lack access to proper treatment.[116] And too many people have been incarcerated for too long for low-level, nonviolent drug crimes. We need to reform our criminal justice system and pursue alternatives to incarceration for low-level and nonviolent drug offenses, and ensure that people get the treatment they need to get back on their feet. We will also foster more collaboration between our public health and criminal justice systems before, during, and after a person is released from prison, to ensure continuity of care for those who suffer from substance use disorders and are arrested and incarcerated.

- **Implement preventive programming for adolescents about drug use and addiction.** We need to do far more as a nation to teach young people, as well as their families, teachers, coaches, mentors, and friends, to intervene early in order to prevent drug and alcohol abuse and addiction. School-based programs that are developmentally appropriate, and community-wide peer mentoring and leadership programs, can be highly effective means of delaying or preventing the first use of alcohol or drugs. That's why we will support states that put in place effective, evidence-based, and locally tailored programs to meet the needs of their residents.

---

116   "New CASA® Report Finds: 65% of All U.S. Inmates Meet Medical Criteria for Substance Abuse Addiction, Only 11% Receive Any Treatment," The National Center on Addiction and Substance Abuse, February 26, 2010.

2.

SAFER TOGETHER

Secure American Leadership and Keep Us Safe

Florida International University Panther Arena on July 23, 2016, in Miami, Florida.

AMERICA IS AN EXCEPTIONAL COUNTRY. Our military is the strongest fighting force in history. Our extensive network of allies reaches around the globe. Our people work harder and dream bigger than anyone else. And, most important, we never stop trying to make the world a better place. We're still, in Lincoln's words, the "last, best hope of earth." That's why, in times of uncertainty and crisis, there's only one place the world looks for leadership: the United States of America. There isn't another country in the world that rivals us.

We know the world can be an unpredictable and dangerous place. On too many mornings Americans have woken up to an act of terrorism in a place no one expected. From Paris and Brussels to San Bernardino and Orlando, our hearts broke for the victims and their families. We came together to mourn, remember, and recommit ourselves to fighting the forces of terror that attack the openness and diversity that define our way of life.

The threat we face from radical jihadists is profound and will continue for years to come. We know we cannot contain ISIS—we must defeat ISIS and the global terrorist movement. And we have learned the hard way that we can score victories over terrorist leaders and networks only to face metastasizing threats down the road. So we also have to play and win the long game, including by having a comprehensive plan to prevent terrorists from ever acquiring nuclear weapons or nuclear materials. That prospect is the gravest national security threat we face.

We'll be firm but wise with our rivals. Our relationship with China is one of the most complicated, as we need to balance efforts to contain Chinese aggression in the global economy and against our partner countries in Asia with the need to cooperate on issues of shared importance, like climate change and global health. Russian aggression has reached levels not seen since the Cold War, as Vladimir Putin is actively pursuing policies to destabilize Eastern Europe and keeping his thumb on the scale in the conflict in Syria. And we must take a distrust-and-verify posture toward Iran following the historic nuclear agreement.

In the coming years, we'll face other global challenges too, from climate change to the threat of nuclear proliferation to Chinese violation of trade rules. The Ebola epidemic laid bare the shortcomings in our global health system. Russian aggression is destabilizing Europe. Cyberattacks are on the rise.

Americans don't cower behind walls. There are those who would turn us into a fearful America that's less secure, less responsible, and less engaged with the world. Instead, we can and must continue to be a strong, confident America that leads the world and keeps our country safe. And we must never lose sight of our strengths as a nation—our dynamic and innovative economy, our open and tolerant society, our democratic values, and our deep and enduring friendships with countries around the world. America is already great. And we will make it even greater.

Retreat is not an option. From fighting international terrorism to combating climate change to stopping human trafficking, no one nation can solve all of these problems alone. We have to work together—and the United States must lead.

To lead, we must maintain the strongest, best-equipped military the world has ever seen. We will pursue a smart and sustainable defense budget driven by strategy—not by the damaging sequester. We will invest in innovation and military capabilities that will allow us to prepare for and fight twenty-first-century threats—all while committing ourselves to a budget that reflects good stewardship of taxpayer dollars.

But our military power is only one part of our strength. To stay on the front lines of solving problems before they threaten us at home, we will embrace all the tools of American power, especially diplomacy and development. Diplomacy is often the only way to avoid a conflict that could end up exacting a much greater cost. It takes patience, persistence, and an eye on the long game—but it's worth it. And that means providing our diplomats with the resources they need to do their jobs, and ensuring that they are safe and secure while doing so. Our diplomatic and development programs make up a small share of our budget, but they provide an outsized benefit to our nation's security, prosperity, and standing in the world.

Finally, we must stay true to our values. That includes standing up to those who call for legalizing torture or hurting civilians just because they're related to suspected terrorists. We need to shore up our alliances and friendships around the world, not undermine them. And we must care for our veterans and military families who have given so much to protect all of us. It is our solemn duty to keep faith with our men and women in uniform, and to consider using military force only as a last resort, not a first choice. Together, we'll make sure that the United States never stops symbolizing freedom, hope, and opportunity to people across the globe.

If the United States leads with purpose and stays true to our principles, we will prevail. We'll stick with our allies to take on the challenges that respect no borders. We'll embrace all the tools of American power— diplomacy, development, defense, and economic statecraft—so we solve problems before they threaten us at home.

To secure American leadership and keep us safe, we will: defeat ISIS and global terrorism; continue to strengthen our alliances and partnerships—and stick with them; be firm but wise with our rivals; keep our military strong and support our veterans and military families; shape the global rules that will keep us safe and make us more prosperous; and stay true to the values that have always made America great.

Defeat ISIS and global terrorism.

–

**Continue to strengthen our alliances
and partnerships—and stick with them.**

–

Be firm but wise with our rivals.

–

**Keep our military strong and support
our veterans and military families.**

–

**Shape the global rules that will keep us safe
and make us more prosperous.**

–

**Stay true to the values that have
always made America great.**

Defeat ISIS and global terrorism.

The terrorist group known as ISIS, which controls a shrinking but still sizable territory in Iraq and Syria, preaches a twisted ideology and a dangerous perversion of Islam. ISIS is attempting a genocide of religious and ethnic minorities. It beheads civilians. It enslaves, tortures, and rapes women and girls. It leads a far-flung network that includes affiliates across the Middle East and North Africa, and sympathizers in Europe, Asia, and even here in North America. It's also part of a broader ideological movement that includes other terrorist groups,[1,2] including Al-Qaeda and affiliates like Boko Haram and al-Nusra.

ISIS operates across three mutually reinforcing dimensions: a physical enclave in Iraq and Syria, an international terrorist network in the region and beyond, and an ideological movement of radical jihadism.[3] We have to target and defeat all three dimensions. And time is of the essence. ISIS is demonstrating new ambition, reach, and capabilities.

---

1 "ISIS Fast Facts," CNN, July 4, 2016, http://www.cnn.com/2014/08/08/world/isis-fast-facts/.
2 Evan Kohlman, "Everything you need to know about ISIS," MSNBC, November 20, 2015, http://www.msnbc.com/msnbc/what-you-need-know-about-isis.
3 Ibid.

We have to break the group's momentum and then its back. We cannot deter or contain ISIS—we have to defeat ISIS.

We should pursue a comprehensive counterterrorism strategy—one that embeds our mission against ISIS within a broader struggle against radical jihadist terrorism that is bigger than any one group, whether it's Al-Qaeda or ISIS or some other network. An immediate war against an urgent enemy and a generational struggle against an ideology with deep roots will not easily be torn out. It will require sustained commitment and every pillar of American power. This is a worldwide fight—and America must lead it.

Our strategy should have three main elements. One: defeat ISIS in Syria, Iraq, and across the Middle East. Two: disrupt and dismantle the global terrorist infrastructure that facilitates the flow of fighters, financing, arms, and propaganda around the world. Three: harden our defenses and those of our allies against external and homegrown threats.

First, we have to take out ISIS's stronghold in Iraq and Syria.

We should intensify the coalition air campaign against its fighters, leaders, and infrastructure; step up support for local Arab and Kurdish forces on the ground and coalition efforts to protect civilians; and pursue a diplomatic strategy aimed at achieving political resolutions to Syria's civil war and Iraq's sectarian divide.

We need an intelligence surge . . . to help us identify and eliminate
ISIS's command and control and its economic lifelines.

What we should not do is to once again put tens of thousands of American ground troops in combat in the Middle East. It's simply not a smart move—and would give ISIS a recruiting field day. If we have learned anything from fifteen years of war in Iraq and Afghanistan, it is that local people and nations have to secure their own communities. We can help them and we should, but we cannot substitute for them. However, we can and should support local and regional ground forces in carrying out this mission. And we should also do more to support Syria's neighbors, especially Jordan and Lebanon, as they take in massive numbers of refugees fleeing both ISIS and Bashar al-Assad, so instability doesn't spread.

Second, we must dismantle the global network of terror that supplies money, arms, propaganda, and fighters. This means targeted efforts to deal with ISIS affiliates, from Libya to Afghanistan. It means going after the key enablers who facilitate illicit financial transactions and help jihadists arrange travel, forge documents, and evade detection.

And it means working with Silicon Valley to wage online battles with extremists to discredit their ideology, expose their lies, and counter their appeals to potential recruits in the West and around the world. We have to do a better job contesting online space, including websites and chat rooms where jihadists communicate with followers. We must deny them virtual territory, just as we deny them actual territory. Online or offline, the bottom line is that we are in a contest of ideas against an ideology of hate—and we have to win it.

Once and for all, the Saudis, the Qataris, and others need to stop their citizens from directly funding extremist organizations, as well as schools and mosques around the world that have set too many young people on a path toward radicalization.[4,5] When it comes to blocking terrorist recruitment, we have to identify the hot spots—the specific neighborhoods and villages, the prisons and schools—where recruitment happens in clusters. Through partnerships with local law enforcement and civil society—especially Muslim community leaders—we have to work to tip the balance away from extremism in these areas.

Third, we must harden our defenses and build our resilience here at home. We need to counter each step in the process that can lead to an attack, deterring would-be terrorists and discovering and disrupting plots before they're carried out.

We know that intelligence gathered and shared by local law enforcement officers is absolutely critical to breaking up plots and preventing attacks. So they need all the resources and support we can give them. And our enemies are constantly adapting, so we have to do the same. We need an intelligence surge—and so do our allies—that includes technical assets, Arabic speakers with deep expertise in the Middle East, and

---

4   Robert Windrem, "Who's Funding ISIS? Wealthy Gulf 'Angel Investors,' Officials Say," NBC, September 21, 2014, http://www.nbcnews.com/storyline/isis-terror/whos-funding-isis-wealthy-gulf-angel-investors-officials-say-n208006.
5   Yousaf Butt, "How Saudi Wahhabism Is the Fountainhead of Islamist Terrorism," *Huffington Post,* January 20, 2015, http://www.huffingtonpost.com/dr-yousaf-butt-/saudi-wahhabism-islam-terrorism_b_6501916.html.

an even closer partnership with regional intelligence services. An intelligence surge would help us identify and eliminate ISIS's command and control and its economic lifelines. We need to enhance our technical surveillance of overseas targets, to effectively intercept terrorist communications, and to fly more reconnaissance missions to track terrorists' movements. And we must find a way to balance legitimate concerns about privacy with the need to combat ISIS and other terrorist groups. There's no magic fix, but we can't just throw up our hands. The tech community and the government have to stop seeing each other as adversaries and start working together to keep Americans safe from terrorists.

Law enforcement also needs the trust of residents and communities, including Muslim Americans. Muslim Americans are working every day on the front lines of the fight against radicalization. We need to empower them. There are millions of Muslims living, working, raising families, and paying taxes in our country. These Americans may be our first, last, and best defense against homegrown radicalization and terrorism. They are the most likely to recognize the insidious effects of radicalization before it's too late and intervene to help set a young person straight. They are the best positioned to block anything going forward.

We should also be vigilant in screening any refugees from Syria, guided by the best judgment of our security professionals in close coordination with our allies and partners. But we cannot allow terrorists to intimidate us into abandoning our values and humanitarian obligations. Turning away orphans, applying a religious test, discriminating against Muslims, slamming the door on every single refugee—that is just not who we are. And we must remember that many of these refugees are fleeing the same terrorists who threaten us. It would be a cruel irony if ISIS can force families from their homes and then also prevent them from ever finding new ones. Our country was founded by people fleeing religious persecution. As George Washington put it, the United States gives "to bigotry no sanction, to persecution no assistance." We cannot, and we will not allow ISIS or other terrorists to undermine these ideals or shake our resolve. America will not cower in fear or hide behind walls. We will lead this fight—and we will succeed.

Combating the threat of nuclear terrorism.

The single gravest national security threat we face is the possibility of terrorists acquiring nuclear material and using it against the United States or our allies.

We must be ready to take on this threat.

We will intensify our efforts to safeguard nuclear material and work with our allies to block nuclear proliferation, not expand it. We need to ensure that no terrorist is ever able to threaten our country or our allies with a weapon of mass destruction.

First, we'll protect nuclear materials and nuclear weapons against theft. The United States has led global efforts to improve nuclear security since the 1990s, but it's time to step up our game. And we should continue to invest in our own security here at home, employing new technologies and improving coordination among federal, state, and local authorities.

Second, we'll prevent the smuggling of nuclear materials using improved export controls, intelligence sharing, and border security systems.

Third, we'll seek to reduce the amount of nuclear material worldwide. This should include negotiating a global ban on producing additional materials for nuclear weapons, and working with other countries to minimize the use of weapons-grade material for civil nuclear programs.

Finally, we'll make clear that any nation or group that supports or enables terrorist efforts to obtain or use weapons of mass destruction will be held accountable. We will be prepared to use direct military action if that's the only way to prevent terrorists from acquiring or using these weapons.

Terrorists involved in the Brussels attacks earlier this year were also monitoring a Belgian nuclear scientist and nuclear plant, a chilling warning that ISIS may be pursuing the sabotage of a nuclear site or acquisition of material to make a dirty bomb. America must lead the world and prevent nuclear weapons or nuclear material from ever falling into the hands of terrorists.

Continue to strengthen our alliances and partnerships—and stick with them.

There are no truly global challenges that can be solved without the United States—and there are no truly global challenges that we can solve on our own. America's network of allies, partners, and friends, from Europe to Asia, forms the backbone of our response to everything from terrorism to climate change.

And we are safer for it. Our allies and partners have stood with us at critical moments. On September 11, 2001, when the United States suffered the worst terrorist attack in our history, our NATO allies invoked Article 5 of the North Atlantic Treaty, which states that an attack against one NATO member is an attack against all, for the first and only time in the organization's history.[6] The following day, newspaper headlines across the European continent proclaimed, "We Are All Americans."[7]

---

6   North Atlantic Treaty Organization, "Collective defence—Article 5," last modified March 22, 2016, http://www.nato.int/cps/en/natohq/topics_110496.htm.
7   Nash Jenkins, "How Paris Stood With the U.S. After 9/11," *Time*, November 14, 2015, http://time.com/4112746/paris-attacks-us-september-911-terrorism/.

Most planes were grounded, but one of the few in the air was carrying the United Kingdom's top national security leaders to Washington, to offer any help they could.[8]

Our friends in Asia work with us to manage the complexities that come from China's rise and deter the threat from North Korea. Our partners in Latin America stand with us in striving to build a lasting peace in our hemisphere. African nations are key partners in the effort to counter global terrorism. Israel is a bastion of security in a region beset by chaos and conflict. Allies and partners extend our reach, share intelligence, provide troops to fight terrorism in places like Afghanistan, offer bases and staging areas around the world for our military, and serve as a bulwark against competitors like Russia and China. And both Moscow and Beijing know our global network of alliances is a significant strategic advantage they can't match.

> *America must not turn its back on the world.*
> *We must strengthen our alliances, not undermine them.*

America must not turn its back on the world. That means we must strengthen our alliances, not undermine them. We must deepen our cooperation with our allies to take on the biggest challenges we face, not turn our backs on decades of partnership. Abandoning our partners would reverse decades of bipartisan American leadership and send a dangerous signal to friend and foe alike.

That is why we will work to strengthen our relationships with our NATO allies, with Israel, and with our partners in Asia and Latin America.

---

8   George Tenet and Bill Harlow, *At the Center of the Storm: My Years at the CIA* (New York: HarperCollins, 2007).

NATO

NATO is one of the best investments America has ever made. From the Balkans to Afghanistan and beyond, NATO allies have fought alongside the United States, sharing our burdens and our sacrifices. In the 1990s, Secretary of Defense William Perry helped guide NATO's expansion based on the alliance's core tenets of collective defense, democracy, consensus, and cooperative security. They became known as the "Perry Principles," and they're still at the heart of what makes NATO the most successful alliance in history.[9]

Today, as we face new and novel threats, we need our allies as much as ever. We need them to be strong and engaged, for they are increasingly on the front lines, particularly in the fight against ISIS. London, Paris, Madrid, Brussels, Istanbul—they've all been hit by terrorism. And, as we saw when a terrorist cell in Hamburg plotted and carried out the September 11 attacks, what happens in Europe has a way of making it to America.[10] That's why it's essential that we have strong partners who can work with us to disrupt plots and dismantle networks in their own countries before they lead to attacks in ours.

European intelligence services should be working hand in hand with our own, including where they may have better reach and expertise as in North Africa. European banks need to crack down on the accounts and the wide range of schemes used to finance terrorist operations. European planes are flying missions over Iraq and Syria, and European special forces are helping train and equip local anti-ISIS forces on the ground. And our NATO allies in Europe are a critical bulwark against Russian aggression.

We need European diplomats and development experts working to improve governance and reduce the appeal of extremism across the wide arc of instability that stretches from West Africa all the way to Asia. Together, we can do more to support moderate voices and stand with

---

9 Ivo H. Daalder, "NATO in the 21st Century: What Purpose? What Missions?", Brookings Institution (1999), p. 54, http://www.brookings.edu/~/media/research/files/reports/1999/4/nato-daalder/reportch3.pdf.
10 "Terrorist cell found in Hamburg where 9/11 attacks conceived," *Daily Telegraph,* October 7, 2009, http://www.telegraph.co.uk/news/worldnews/europe/germany/6267615/Terrorist-cell-found-in-Hamburg-where-911-attacks-conceived.html.

Tunisians, Libyans, Kurds, and others in the region who are trying to do the right thing and build open, moderate, peaceful communities.

And we need to support our European partners—helping them improve intelligence and law enforcement, facilitating information-sharing, working more closely at every level. The most urgent task is stopping the flow of foreign fighters to and from the Middle East. Thousands of young recruits have flocked to Syria from France, Germany, Belgium, and the United Kingdom.[11] Their European passports make it easier for them to cross borders and eventually return home, radicalized and battle-hardened. We need to know the identities of every fighter who makes that trip and start revoking passports and visas.

Stemming this tide will require much better coordination among every country along the way. Right now, many European nations do not alert one another when they turn away a suspected jihadist at the border or when a passport is stolen. And we must work with Turkey, a NATO ally, to control the border where foreign fighters cross into Syria.[12]

The NATO alliance has delivered unprecedented peace and prosperity on both sides of the Atlantic since it began—and it remains one of the best tools we have for tackling the challenges we face as a nation and a world.

11   Jessica Stern and J.M. Berger, "ISIS and the Foreign Fighter Phenomenon," *Atlantic*, March 8, 2015, http://www.theatlantic.com/international/archive/2015/03/isis-and-the-foreign-fighter-problem/387166/.
12   Greg Miller and Souad Mekhennet, "Undercover teams, increased surveillance and hardened borders: Turkey cracks down on foreign fighters," *Washington Post*, March 6, 2016, https://www.washingtonpost.com/world/national-security/undercover-teams-increased-surveillance-and-hardened-borders-turkey-cracks-down-on-foreign-fighters/2016/03/06/baa4ba3a-e219-11e5-8d98-4b3d9215ade1_story.html.

Israel and the Middle East

In this unsettled time, Israel needs a strong America by its side—and America needs a strong and secure Israel by ours. It is in America's national interest for Israel to remain a bastion of security and a core partner in a region that is mired in chaos. It's in our interest for Israel to be strong enough to deter its enemies and committed to taking steps in the pursuit of peace.

The rising tide of extremism across the wide arc of instability from North Africa to South Asia, the continued aggression of Iran, and the growing effort to delegitimize Israel on the world stage all make our partnership with Israel more indispensable than ever. We have to develop a common strategic vision and pursue a coordinated approach, deepen cooperation and consultation across the board, and take our relationship to the next level.

In recent years, the United States has worked with Israel to support the development of the Iron Dome air defense system, which saved many Israeli lives when Hamas rockets began to fly from Gaza. Now, we need to take our partnership further to ensure that Israel continues to maintain its Qualitative Military Edge (QME), including by inviting the Israeli Prime Minister to the White House in our first month in office. The United States should help further bolster Israeli air defenses, including to cover Israel's north, and we should make it a top priority to develop better tunnel detection, technology to prevent arms smuggling and kidnapping.

We remain convinced that peace is possible between Israelis and Palestinians, and we refuse to give up on the goal of two states for two peoples. Inaction is not an option and a one-state solution is no solution; it is a prescription for endless conflict. Israelis deserve security, recognition, and a normal life free from terror. And Palestinians should be able to govern themselves in their own state in peace and dignity. As difficult as it is, we need to look for opportunities to move forward together. Everyone has to do their part to create the conditions for progress by taking positive actions that can rebuild trust and by avoiding damaging actions, including with respect to settlements.

Today in the Middle East, Israel and its Arab neighbors find that many of their strategic interests are increasingly aligned. That creates room for greater coordination. Neither Israel nor its Arab neighbors want to see Iran increase its influence in the region or violent jihadists gain greater footholds. We should encourage more intelligence sharing and security cooperation, and broader diplomatic engagement. And the United States must continue to work with our Arab partners in the Gulf—countries like Jordan, which is sheltering hundreds of thousands of refugees fleeing the war in Syria, is flying combat missions against ISIS, and has lost soldiers in the fight. Such partnerships are vital for America's security and for the stability of the entire region.

Israel and the United States are two nations woven together, lands built by immigrants and exiles seeking to live and worship in freedom, given life by democratic principles, and sustained by the service and sacrifice of generations of patriots. And at our best, Israel and America both are seen as a "light unto nations" because of those values—an ideal we must continuously strive to achieve together.

Asia

Sixty percent of the world's population lives in Asia.[13] More than half of commercial shipping passes through Asian oceans and waterways.[14] Just as the twentieth century was dominated by the United States' relationship with Europe, the twenty-first century will be America's Pacific Century. That's why we must work to make sure America's alliances, economic ties, diplomacy, and military role in Asia are stronger than they've ever been.

We strengthened our existing alliances with close partners like South Korea and Japan, and established new relationships. We helped to put Burma on the path to democracy, and it has just undergone its first peaceful democratic transition, demonstrating the valuable role that American leadership can play in the world. We worked to counter the threat of a belligerent North Korea, and when diplomacy fell short, brought the strongest sanctions ever against its dangerous weapons programs alongside our regional partners. And because of these stronger ties, we were able to stand up to China wherever our interests dictated: In the South China Sea over freedom of navigation; on its violation of human rights; and to protect American companies from costly intellectual property theft.

As the fastest-growing region in the world with a rising middle class, Asia is arguably the most important twenty-first-century market for American goods, and American businesses must have access to Asia if they are to succeed. From 2009 to 2012, U.S. exports to China increased by $40 billion, and exports to Asia as a whole rose by $120 billion.[15,16] Some 3.5 million American jobs are supported by exports to Asia.[17]

The U.S.-China relationship is one of the most complex and consequential in the world, and managing it requires acting wisely and firmly.

---

13 Ana Swanson, "5 ways the world will look dramatically different in 2100," *Washington Post,* August 17, 2015, https://www.washingtonpost.com/news/wonk/wp/2015/08/17/5-ways-the-world-will-look-dramatically-different-in-2100/.
14 Asia Maritime Transparency Initiative, "18 Maps that Explain Maritime Security in Asia," last modified summer 2014, https://amti.csis.org/atlas/.
15 "Trade in Goods with China," U.S. Census Bureau, 2016, https://www.census.gov/foreign-trade/balance/c5700.html.
16 "Trade in Goods with Asia," U.S. Census Bureau, 2016, https://www.census.gov/foreign-trade/balance/c0016.html.
17 "Employment and Trade," International Trade Administration, 2016, http://www.trade.gov/mas/ian/employment/.

Maintaining strong alliances and developing new partnerships in Asia will be essential to managing China on issues from trade to the South China Sea. We will work through platforms like ASEAN to strengthen our relationships with Southeast Asian nations, including Thailand, Vietnam, and Indonesia, and continue to support Burma's transition to a more open society.

Maintaining strong alliances in Asia is critical for protecting the security of the United States. Take the threat posed by North Korea—perhaps the most repressive regime on the planet, run by a sadistic dictator who wants to develop long-range missiles that could carry a nuclear weapon to the United States. We worked closely with our allies Japan and South Korea to respond to this threat, including by creating a missile defense system that stands ready to shoot down a North Korean warhead, should its leaders ever be reckless enough to launch one at us.[18] The technology is America's. Key parts of it are located on Japanese ships. All three countries contributed to it. And this year all three of our militaries ran a joint drill to test it. That's the power of allies.

---

18 KJ Kwon and Dugald McConnell, "South Korea, Japan to join U.S. for missile-defense exercise," CNN, May 17, 2016, http://www.cnn.com/2016/05/16/asia/south-korea-japan-missile-defense-exercise/.

The Americas

Too often in foreign policy, America looks east, we look west, but we don't always look north and south. No region in the world is more important to our long-term prosperity and security than Latin America. No ally is closer to America, culturally and strategically, than our friends in Canada. And no region in the world is better positioned to emerge as a new force for global peace and progress.

America's ties with Mexico are particularly close. About 65 percent of the 50 million Latinos who live in the United States have Mexican descent.[19] More than 1 million American citizens live in Mexico.[20] These deep cultural ties, and the 2,000-mile-long border we share, mean that Mexico's ongoing security challenges matter to the United States. The best way to keep America safe is by working together with Mexico on shared security threats, so we can stop those threats before they reach our border. That includes improving cooperation and intelligence sharing to improve anti-narcotics efforts and address other security challenges.

We should also be looking for every opportunity to collaborate with our regional partners in the fight against climate change. The United States trades more energy with Canada and Mexico than with the rest of the world combined, and we have a deeply connected electric grid and energy system. It makes sense for our three countries to work in concert to combat climate change, build twenty-first-century energy infrastructure, and accelerate the transition to a clean energy future. That's why we will negotiate a North American Climate Compact with the leaders of Canada and Mexico that includes ambitious national targets for cutting carbon pollution, coordinated policy approaches to energy efficiency, vehicle efficiency, and methane pollution, and strong labor and environmental standards for energy infrastructure.

The historic restoration of diplomatic relations between the United States and Cuba has opened up new possibilities throughout the region. The decision to restore relations and move toward normalization was

---

19 "Statistical Portrait of Hispanics in the United States," Pew Research Center, April 19, 2016, http://www .pewhispanic.org/2016/04/19/statistical-portrait-of-hispanics-in-the-united-states-key-charts/.

20 "U.S. Relations with Mexico," U.S. Department of State, July 12, 2016, http://www.state.gov/r/pa/ei/bgn/35749.htm.

the result of years of hard work, diplomacy, and tense negotiations—and the recognition that our long-standing policy of isolating Cuba was only serving to strengthen the Castros' grip on power.

Now we need to continue moving forward, opening up travel, business, and civil society relations between our countries. If we go backward, no one will benefit more than the hard-liners in Havana. In fact, there may be no stronger argument for engagement than the fact that Cuba's hard-liners are so opposed to it. They don't want strong connections with the United States. They don't want Cuban Americans traveling to the island. They don't want American students, clergy, and NGO activists interacting with the Cuban people. That's precisely why we need to do it.

Those who think of Latin America as a land of crime and coups are sorely misinformed. Latin America is home to vibrant democracies, expanding middle classes, abundant energy supplies, and a combined GDP of more than $5 trillion.[21,22] Our economies, communities, and even our families are deeply intertwined. The United States needs to build on the "power of proximity." Closer ties across Latin America will help our economy at home and strengthen our hand around the world, especially in the Asia-Pacific.

We have work to do together to take on the persistent challenges in our hemisphere, from crime to drugs to poverty, and to stand in defense of our shared values against oppressive regimes. And we have to work together, too, to build on the opportunities we all share, including in clean energy and the fight against climate change. Latin American countries were leaders in forging the historic 195-nation Paris climate agreement last year.[23] They have been pioneering new approaches to building cleaner, more sustainable economies because they recognize that climate change poses an imminent threat to their economies, their security, and the health of their communities.

The United States needs to lead in the Americas—because if we don't, others will.

---

21 "Latin America and Caribbean Overview," The World Bank, 2016, http://www.worldbank.org/en/region/lac/overview.

22 "Latin America & Caribbean," The World Bank, 2016, http://data.worldbank.org/region/latin-america-and-caribbean.

23 "Latin American leadership is critical to securing a Paris climate pact," Climate Home, November 28, 2015, http://www.climatechangenews.com/2015/11/28/latin-american-leadership-critical-to-securing-a-paris-climate-pact/.

Africa

With forty-nine religiously, ethnically, and culturally diverse countries, including some of the fastest-growing economies in the world, Africa is increasingly important to the United States.

The days of Africa being seen as only a recipient of aid are behind us. Instead, we will seek new and dynamic partnerships with African countries to help accelerate the advances that are already underway in many parts of the continent and collaborate to reverse dangerous trends in other areas by encouraging political, economic, and social progress. We will also build on the work of the Obama administration to promote U.S. private sector investment in clean-energy projects and sustainable development across Africa.

While several African nations have made important advances in strengthening their democratic institutions, democracy is under pressure across much of Africa. Too many people still live under rulers who care too much about the longevity of their reign and too little about the legacy of their country's future. We will continue working to promote good governance, including free, fair, and transparent elections; a free media; independent judiciaries; accountable and legitimate institutions; and the protection of human rights.

And we must remain committed to working with our friends and allies across the region to push back against extremism, from Boko Haram in Nigeria to al Shabab in Somalia to ISIS in Libya. We will work toward a negotiated solution to all of the continent's long-standing conflicts, but the responsibility for fixing what ails the region lies first and foremost with the people themselves.

Finally, we will also continue to make long-term economic investments that are sustainable and beneficial to the African people, not just the political elites, including efforts to revitalize agriculture and strengthen food security, improve health care and health systems, and foster innovative approaches to expanding access to capital and information.

Be firm but wise with our rivals.

When America doesn't lead, we leave a vacuum—and our rivals are keen to fill it.

China seeks to challenge our interests and international rules as it grows in power, but can also play an important role in working with the United States and the international community on shared challenges. Our relationship with China is complex and requires steady, wise stewardship. Our challenge is to expand cooperation where our interests overlap—and manage competition to ensure it is constructive, not destructive, and that China abides by international rules and norms.

Russia presents a more difficult relationship following Putin's aggressive military action in Ukraine, interference in elections, cyberattacks, and propping up of Assad in Syria. We must be firm in challenging Putin's aggression and standing with our allies and partners in the face of Putin's destabilizing actions. At the same time, we need to continue to find ways to cooperate with Russia on issues that are in our interest, like implementation of the Iran nuclear deal.

These are real challenges, but the United States must never forget our advantages. We have the world's strongest and most dynamic economy. We are uniquely capable of forging diplomatic solutions and bringing other countries to our side in disputes. Our society is more diverse, open, and resilient than any in the world. And our deeply held alliances, partnerships, and friendships with nations on every continent make us even stronger.

The key is to never forget who we are dealing with—not friends or allies, but countries that share some common interests with the United States amid many disagreements.

These are complex relationships. For instance, China's growth has reshaped the global economy and affected the balance of power in Asia. The Chinese frequently test international rules and norms around cybersecurity and military activity in the South China Sea and consistently seek opportunities to expand their influence in Africa and Latin America—but they are absolutely essential diplomatic partners in the global fight against climate change.

That's why it's essential we use all of the tools of American power, especially diplomacy, development, and economic statecraft, to deal with our rivals. While we believe our military must continue to be the best-trained, best-equipped fighting force in the world, we equally believe that military action must be a last resort. That's what it means to be strong and smart in engaging with our rivals.

China

The U.S.-China relationship is a deeply complicated one. The United States and China can and must cooperate on areas like climate change and nuclear nonproliferation. On national security, we need strong and steady leadership to stand up to Beijing on issues like North Korea's nuclear program, the South China Sea, and cybersecurity. And we must stand tough in the U.S.-China economic relationship—and work to deliver fair outcomes for American workers and consumers.

We won't get fair trade with China by hurling insults or blowing up both economies. We won't deter China from its belligerence in the South China Sea or prevent North Korea from acquiring a nuclear weapon through meaningless bluster. We won't expand the scope of human dignity for the Chinese people through ignorance.

Fundamentally, the United States' relationship with China must aim to manage competition while expanding cooperation, and work to bind the Chinese to operate by international rules and norms rather than allowing them to bend and subvert them.

That means we will aggressively monitor product dumping and production surges from China, especially in sensitive sectors like steel, and use every tool we have to combat these efforts to undercut American workers. When China denies market access to U.S. companies, we will adopt a policy of reciprocity and restrict Chinese access in the same areas. And we will say "no" to China's petition for market economy status. A country with massive state-owned enterprises and a track record of currency manipulation should not be granted a trade status that will make it easier for them to undercut legal protections for American workers and companies. And we will consider the full range of options for responding to Chinese currency manipulation, including tariffs and other remedies.

The United States has a deep and abiding interest in the South China Sea and to the free flow of commerce—so critical to our economy—that moves through it. We welcome the recent UN ruling on the territorial disputes in the region, and believe all claimants need to abide by the ruling and continue to pursue peaceful, multilateral means to resolve disputes. We will work with our allies to counter Chinese aggression in the South

China Sea, including by strengthening the capacity of our regional partners[24] and conducting regular operations to ensure freedom of navigation.

We will hold China accountable for cyberattacks and violating our cybersecurity agreement, and seek sanctions against companies and individuals who benefit from cyber espionage. And we will not let up in our efforts to push China to respect human rights, including the rights of Tibetans, and we will continue to support efforts to peacefully resolve cross-strait issues between China and Taiwan.

There are also areas where we need to seek greater cooperation with China. The United States and China are the two biggest global emitters of the greenhouse gases that drive climate change, and so our two countries have a unique responsibility in solving the climate crisis.[25] After years of distrust and limited action on the part of the Chinese, President Obama and Chinese President Xi Jinping achieved a historic breakthrough when they jointly announced elements of the United States' and China's national goals to combat climate change in the lead-up to the UN climate summit in Paris.[26] The United States and China have launched multiple joint efforts to develop clean energy technologies, cut superpollutants like black carbon and methane, and recognize the leadership of cities and other sub-national actors in both countries in combating climate change.[27] This work is vital to addressing the climate crisis and spurring action from other major polluters, like India and Brazil.

24   CNN Philippines Staff, "What you need to know about EDCA," CNN Philippines, April 14, 2016, http://cnnphilippines.com/news/2016/01/13/what-you-need-to-know-about-edca.html.
25   "Global Greenhouse Gas Emissions Data," U.S. Environmental Protection Agency, 2016, https://www3.epa.gov/climatechange/ghgemissions/global.html.
26   "FACT SHEET: President Xi Jinping's State Visit to the United States," White House Office of the Press Secretary, September 25, 2015, https://www.whitehouse.gov/the-press-office/2015/09/25/fact-sheet-president-xi-jinpings-state-visit-united-states.
27   Melanie Hart, Pete Ogden, and Kelly Sims Gallagher, "Green Finance: The Next Frontier for U.S.-China Climate Cooperation," Center for American Progress, June 13, 2016, https://www.americanprogress.org/issues/security/report/2016/06/13/139276/green-finance-the-next-frontier-for-u-s-china-climate-cooperation/.

Russia

Since the collapse of the Soviet Union, we have sought a modern, developed, prosperous Russia that abides by international rules and acts as a constructive presence on the world stage. Republican and Democratic administrations alike worked to integrate the Russian government into global institutions, Russian businesses into the global economy, and Russian society into global scientific, educational, cultural, and civil society networks.

Unfortunately, under the leadership of Vladimir Putin, Russia is pursuing policies that threaten European security and the broader global order. Russia is actively working to destabilize the former Soviet states on its borders, violating Ukraine's sovereignty, and putting pressure on our NATO allies. And Russia is actively working to undermine international rules and U.S. interests around the world.

We must be clear-eyed about Russian aggression, and be prepared to unflinchingly stand up to it. As long as Russia remains on a course of belligerent, anti-Western policies, the United States must work with our allies and partners to deter and contain them.

That means we need to focus on stopping Russian aggression in the near term. That's why it's essential that we maintain our support for our NATO partners. We need to encourage our European allies and partners to invest more in their own national defense. And we need to take steps to shore up our non-NATO partners in Eastern Europe and Central Asia, including helping them defend their sovereignty, improve governance at home, and grow their economies.

We must also take steps to help Europe build a stronger energy system that is less dependent on Russian oil and gas. Russia's stranglehold on European energy supplies complicates any effort to contain its aggressive behavior. We will work to help Europe diversify its energy mix and sources.

Even as we work to contain Russian aggression, there are areas where we must engage in smart diplomacy. We should work with Russian leaders on issues of vital and shared interest, including arms control, nuclear nonproliferation, and nuclear security, as when the United States successfully negotiated the New START treaty to continue reducing nuclear weapons arsenals. And we need to work to convince Russia to be a partner, not a roadblock, in moving toward a diplomatic solution to the civil war in Syria that paves the way for new leadership and enables Syrians from every community to take on ISIS.

Iran

When President Obama took office in 2009, Iran was racing toward a nuclear weapon. They had mastered the nuclear fuel cycle—meaning that they had the material, scientists, and technical know-how to create material for nuclear weapons. They had produced and installed thousands of centrifuges, expanded their secret facilities, established a robust uranium enrichment program, and defied their international obligations under the Nuclear Non-Proliferation Treaty. And they weren't feeling the consequences.[28]

Through a two-pronged strategy of pressure and engagement, we made clear to the Iranians that the door to diplomacy was open—if they answered the concerns of the international community in a serious and credible way. At the same time, we increased pressure on the regime, systematically increasing our military capabilities in the region and building the global coalition that produced some of the most effective, far-reaching economic sanctions in history, largely cutting Iran off from the world's economic and financial system.[29]

The Obama administration worked with Congress and the European Union to put the sanctions in place. And one by one, we persuaded energy-hungry consumers of Iranian oil like India and South Korea to cut back. Soon, Iran's tankers sat rusting in port. Its economy was collapsing.

These new measures were effective because we made them global. American sanctions provided the foundation, but Iran didn't really feel the heat until we turned this into an international campaign so biting that it had no choice but to negotiate. They could no longer play off one country against another. They had no place to hide.

That's the power of alliances—and that's how America reached the historic nuclear agreement with Iran last year.

---

28 David Sanger and William Broad, "U.S. and Allies Warn Iran Over Nuclear Deception," *New York Times*, September 25, 2009, http://www.nytimes.com/2009/09/26/world/middleeast/26nuke.html.
29 United Nations Security Council, "Security Council Imposes Additional Sanctions on Iran, Voting 12 in Favour to 2 Against, with 1 Abstention," June 9, 2010, http://www.un.org/press/en/2010/sc9948.doc.htm.

The Iran nuclear deal isn't perfect—but it's strong and it's comprehensive. If vigorously enforced, it blocks every pathway for Iran to get a bomb.[30] And it gives us better tools for verification, inspection, and compelling rigorous compliance with the terms of the deal.

Without a deal, Iran's breakout time—the length of time they need to produce enough material for a nuclear weapon—would be a couple of months. With the deal, that breakout time stretches to a year, which means that if Iran cheats, we'll know it and we'll have time to respond decisively.

Without a deal, we would have no credible inspections of Iran's nuclear facilities. With a deal, we'll have unprecedented access. We'll be able to monitor every aspect of their nuclear program.

But ultimately, whether this deal succeeds or fails depends on the next President. Our posture toward the Iranians will be: distrust and verify. Iran will test the next President, try to see how far they can bend the rules. We can't let them. That means penalties even for small violations. It means keeping our allies onboard—but being willing to snap back sanctions into place unilaterally if we have to. And it means working with Congress to close any gaps in the sanctions.

We must tell Iran loudly and clearly: the United States will never allow them to acquire a nuclear weapon. And we will take whatever actions are necessary to protect the United States and our allies, including military action if Iran attempts to obtain a nuclear weapon.

But the nuclear deal alone is not sufficient. We will continue enforcing non-nuclear sanctions as we deal with Iran's broader efforts to destabilize the region. We will deepen America's commitment to Israel's security, reaffirm that the Persian Gulf is a region of vital interest to the United States, maintain a robust military presence in the region, and deepen our intelligence cooperation with our Gulf allies. We will also build a coalition to counter Iran's proxies, particularly Hezbollah. And we cannot be idle in the face of Iran's abuses at home, from its detention of political prisoners to its crackdown on freedom of expression, including online. America will enforce and, if need be, broaden our human rights sanctions.

---

30 William Broad and Sergio Peçanha, "The Iran Nuclear Deal—A Simple Guide," *New York Times,* January 15, 2016, http://www.nytimes.com/interactive/2015/03/31/world/middleeast/simple-guide-nuclear-talks-iran-us.html.

Keep our military strong and support our veterans and military families.

Keeping America safe must be our number one priority. To defend our homeland, protect our global interests, deter our adversaries, and continue securing the free movement of global trade and navigation, we must ensure the United States has the world's strongest and most capable military—now and in the future. The United States must be the world's partner, not its policeman. That is why we will strengthen our network of military alliances and work with our friends to build security across the world. But, if necessary, we must also be prepared to take military action to protect Americans and our vital interests.

We know that force and diplomacy must complement each other, not compete with each other. We must be smart and tough when it comes to using America's military might—never reckless. We cannot send our armed forces into a fight without a clear objective, and a plan to achieve it. And military force must be a last resort, not a first choice.

Supporting our veterans is a sacred responsibility. Fulfilling that responsibility ensures that veterans receive the opportunity, care, and support they earned by serving our country. Prioritizing their reintegration also ensures that they bring their unique skills and experience to the success of their communities and our nation after their service is over. Yet too often, we as a nation have failed to uphold our end of the bargain. We must continue to support the needs and talents of all who have served and who serve us still, whether soldiers, sailors, marines, airmen, or coast guardsmen, including active duty, reserve, and National Guard, and every race, creed, gender, and sexual orientation.

We are stronger when we work with our allies around the world and care for our veterans here at home.

Specifically, we need to:

- **Build a defense strategy based on smart power, predictable budgets, and modern tools.** The U.S. military plays an essential role in deterring conflict. Our global capabilities and the forward posture of our forces help support our allies and partners, deter aggression, and provide a platform for responding quickly and effectively to crises of all kinds. As America's men and women in uniform are asked to risk their lives to defend and advance our core national interests, every effort must be made to ensure they remain the best-trained and -equipped force on any battlefield. That's why we need a stable and predictable defense budget set according to strategic need rather than unrealistic budget caps. We will put forward a defense spending plan that emphasizes smart, sustainable investments and dedicates the resources necessary to recruit, retain, and support our all-volunteer force. We will aggressively pursue reforms in procurement and acquisitions, personnel, military readiness, and management that will reduce waste and redundancy and make sure our military remains the most agile, innovative, strongest fighting force in the world.

- **Fundamentally reform veterans' health care to ensure veterans' access to timely and quality health care and block efforts to privatize the Veterans Health Administration.** The VA healthcare scandal, and the news that long wait times for appointments at VA hospitals may have contributed to the deaths of as many as 1,000 veterans, was an outrage. Veterans must have access to a system that puts their needs first. But in order to build such a system, prepared for the unique and growing needs of the twenty-first century, we cannot simply throw more money at the problem or tell veterans to go get private care.[31] We also cannot throw our veterans at the mercy of the private insurance system without any care coordination, or leave them to fend for themselves with healthcare providers who have no expertise in the unique challenges facing veterans. Choice should be a part of the solution, but the VA must maintain the ultimate responsibility of coordinating and ensuring comprehensive and quality health care for every veteran and the specialized services they deserve, including world-class mental health and counseling services to treat the invisible, latent, and toxic wounds of war. We also have to ensure that our women veterans are fully and equally served by the VA. The Veterans Health Administration must embrace comprehensive process and systems integration across its healthcare enterprise to ensure a fully networked and financially sustainable organization that is dedicated to best practices and continual improvement in everything it does.

- **Modernize and refocus the full spectrum of veterans' benefits across the federal government.** In the years following World War II, 16 million returning servicemembers were able to rely on the healthcare and educational opportunities afforded by an adaptable VA organization, headed at the time by General Omar Bradley.[32] General Bradley worked effectively with Congress and stakeholders to build the system that cared for those returning troops. And we must do the same to streamline and modernize the veterans' benefits system today. This includes

---

31 Jerry Moran and Markwayne Mullin, "VA Choice Program must work better for our veterans," *The Hill,* May 12, 2015, http://thehill.com/opinion/op-ed/241458-va-choice-program-must-work-better-for-our-veterans.
32 "History and Timeline," U.S. Department of Veterans Affairs, 2016, http://www.benefits.va.gov/gibill/history .asp; "History—VA History," U.S. Department of Veterans Affairs, 2016, http://www.va.gov/about_va/vahistory.asp.

streamlining and simplifying the claims process to end the disability benefits and appeals backlog and conducting an end-to-end evaluation to optimize the full scope of benefits afforded to our vets.

- **Overhaul VA governance to create a new veteran-centric model of excellence.** Fulfilling the nation's duty of taking care of our veterans requires effective performance by the VA and other federal agencies that support veterans. We must reform management within the Department of Veterans Affairs, ensure fair and transparent accountability, and ensure the VA has budget certainty by ending the sequester and prioritizing full funding and advance appropriations for the entire Department of Veterans Affairs.

- **Empower veterans and strengthen our economy and communities by connecting their unique skills to the jobs of the future.** America's veterans are an enormous asset for the future of the country and our economic growth. Veterans bring unique skills from their time in the military that can move America's economy forward. From their commitment to service and teamwork to specific job skills from computer science to welding, investment in our veterans can power a workforce for the future. We must support and broaden initiatives that provide educational benefits and job training for veterans, and we need to do more to help our veteran entrepreneurs. We have to protect veterans from discrimination and predatory companies that unfairly target veterans and their families. And we should work to expand complementary programs and services to end veterans homelessness and recognize the honorable service of LGBT veterans.

- **Sustain and strengthen the all-volunteer force.** The All-Volunteer Force (AVF) has been stressed by fifteen years of continuous combat and is endeavoring to rebuild and reset, while facing growing instability and complexity around the world, reduced end strength, and an uncertain fiscal environment. We need to develop a broad strategy on Department of Defense budget and reform measures grounded in permanently ending the damaging sequester while making smart reforms in both defense and nondefense spending. We must also promote total force readiness through smart compensation and benefits reform and adopting modern and inclusive personnel policies, including welcoming women to compete for all military positions and aggressively combating military sexual assault and harassment.

- **Strengthen services and support for military families.** Military family readiness is a critical part of total force readiness. Military families face unique concerns and challenges, especially after fifteen years of continuous deployments. To tackle these challenges, we will support military spouses in continuing their educations, finding jobs, building careers, and securing their financial futures—and we'll do more to help our servicemen and -women and their spouses balance the demands of work and family by increasing flexibility, supporting childcare, and improving family leave policies. We need to do more to make certain that the children of military families receive a world-class education from cradle to college. We should also champion efforts to care for our military members and families, including enhancing DoD programs that focus on mental health issues, remaining committed to extended leave policies, and supporting Gold Star families.[33]

The next President must be committed to a strong and resilient military, built by the extraordinary men and women who volunteer to serve and the families who serve alongside them.

---

33 "Gold Star Survivors," U.S. Army, 2016, https://www.army.mil/goldstar/.

Shape the global rules
and institutions that will keep us safe
and make us more prosperous.

After the Second World War, the United States and our allies set out to secure lasting peace and prosperity and prevent another global conflagration. To accomplish these goals, we began building the institutions that now make up the international order—the United Nations, the International Monetary Fund, and the World Bank. Our allies began the long, hard road of creating a more deeply integrated Europe. We set up NATO and signed treaties to ensure that should conflict break out again, despite our highest hopes, none of us would be left standing alone.

These new rules, agreements, and institutions promoted global cooperation, fostered historic economic growth, and helped spread democracy. However, these institutions are all under new strains, and are being challenged by Russian and Chinese aggression—and we need to recommit ourselves not just to securing peace for the world, but to making sure the international order works for the American people.

We live in a world that is increasingly interconnected. When the United Kingdom voted to leave the European Union earlier this year, the consequent stock market turmoil impacted Americans' retirement accounts.[34] The Ebola epidemic in Guinea, Sierra Leone, and Liberia killed thousands of people in West Africa—and the small number of cases that emerged among people in other countries who had recently been working in the region laid bare how our system of international air travel could easily spread a more infectious disease to millions.[35] Countries like China and Russia compete to exert their influence and gain political sway in emerging markets in Africa, South America, and Asia.

What's more, this is an era in which tackling global challenges will require truly global solutions. Although the United States is the second-largest emitter of the greenhouse gases that cause climate change, and the biggest emitter per capita, we account for only about 16 percent of emissions globally.[36] In other words, we cannot solve the climate crisis on our own.

To create a strong economy at home and to keep our country and our families safe, America cannot retreat from the world—we must lead. We must make sure the international system is working to America's advantage, rather than against American interests. That means working to shape a truly fair twenty-first-century international economic system that supports strong growth and protects American workers from unfair practices; leading the global fight against climate change, which knows no borders; addressing emerging threats from health pandemics and cyberattacks; and continuing to counter the threat of nuclear proliferation.

34   Dan Burns, "Good Morning America: Britain just voted out of the EU . . . What's that mean for America?" Reuters, June 24, 2016, http://www.reuters.com/article/us-britain-eu-usa-q-a-idUSKCN0ZA21Y.

35   James Gallager, "Ebola outbreak: How many people have died?", BBC, October 15, 2014, http://www.bbc.com/news/health-29628481.

36   Matt McGrath, "China's per capita carbon emissions overtake EU's," BBC News, September 21, 2014, http://www.bbc.com/news/science-environment-29239194.

Building a fair international economic system.

Building an economy that works for everyone, not just those at the top, requires that we invest in creating more good-paying jobs here at home and rewrite the rules so American corporations invest in their workers rather than shipping jobs overseas. But the American economy does not exist in a bubble. Although exports of American goods and services support more than 11 million jobs, globalization and trade have not delivered for American workers the way they were supposed to.[37]

We need to make the global economy work for American families. That means we need to rewrite the rules of the global economy so that other countries don't have the incentive or the opportunity to undercut the kind of wage, labor, and environmental standards that help our middle class thrive and keep our communities safe and healthy.[38]

To do that, we cannot let countries with state-owned enterprises, like China, take advantage of the international system. It's unfair to businesses that work hard and play by the rules to be trying to compete against companies that are heavily subsidized by their home governments. And we need only one word to answer China's petition for so-called market economy status, being considered right now: No. If China gains market economy status it would defang our anti-dumping laws and allow China to flood American markets with cheap goods, further undercutting our businesses.

And we have to crack down on the wealthy and big corporations that use tricks and shell games to hide their money in overseas tax shelters. The release of the "Panama Papers" this year showed just how widespread this practice is among the super-rich. They are skipping out on paying their fair share in taxes and sheltering trillions of dollars in their secret offshore tax havens.[39] By not paying their fair share, they are undermining our economy and our democratic system and shirking their responsibility to the country that helped make them successful in the first place.

---

37 "Employment and Trade," International Trade Administration, 2016, http://www.trade.gov/mas/ian/employment/.
38 Lucy Hornby and Shawn Donnan, "China fights for market economy status," *Financial Times,* May 9, 2016, https://next.ft.com/content/572f435e-0784-11e6-9b51-0fb5e65703ce.
39 "Panama Papers: Huge leak alleges elites hiding money," al Jazeera, April 6, 2016, http://www.aljazeera.com/news/2016/04/data-leak-reveals-world-wealthy-hide-money-160403192018665.html.

We need to work cooperatively with our allies in Europe and Latin America to tackle tax avoidance and set global rules so the biggest companies and wealthiest families aren't able to escape paying their fair share by playing shell games or incorporating overseas. We will explore options for increasing requirements on shell companies to disclose details of beneficial ownership to crack down on tax avoidance. And we won't ignore the shell companies in our own backyard, either. We need to strengthen rules to prevent U.S. states from being used to shelter foreign assets or avoid paying taxes. Simply put, there should not be one system for working families and another for the super-rich—and we won't stand for it any longer.

Combating climate change.

Climate change is real, it is being driven by human activity, and it is happening right now. Fifteen of the sixteen hottest years on record have occurred in this century, and 2016 is on track to break all the records once again. Communities from Baltimore to Virginia Beach to Miami are experiencing more frequent flooding as a result of sea level rise.[40,41] The West has been parched by a historic drought. The same pattern is repeating in countries around the world. Rising seas pose an existential threat to low-lying Pacific island nations and countries like Bangladesh. Africa's Sahel region has endured brutal droughts and food shortages. Snowpacks that historically provided year-round water for drinking and agriculture in places like the Andes are retreating. The Pentagon calls climate change a "threat multiplier" that can further destabilize already turbulent conditions, increasing the likelihood of conflicts over scarce resources like water and food, and fueling social and political unrest.

As the world's biggest and most powerful economy—and as the second-biggest emitter of greenhouse gases and the biggest historical emitter—the United States has a responsibility to lead the global response to the climate challenge.[42] By making strong progress to reduce greenhouse gas emissions at home, President Obama had sufficient leverage to pressure other major emitters, like China and India, to step up and change how they did business. This dual process where domestic policy changes helped spur international action led to the historic 195-nation Paris climate agreement, the first in our history where every country agreed to be part of the climate solution.[43]

But while the Paris agreement is critical, it is not sufficient. To keep global warming below the 2-degrees-Celsius threshold and avoid the

---

40 "NASA, NOAA Analyses Reveal Record-Shattering Global Warm Temperatures in 2015," NASA, last modified January 20, 2016, http://www.nasa.gov/press-release/nasa-noaa-analyses-reveal-record-shattering-global-warm-temperatures-in-2015.
41 Baden Copeland, Josh Keller, and Bill Marsh, "What Could Disappear," *New York Times*, April 24, 2016, http://www.nytimes.com/interactive/2012/11/24/opinion/sunday/what-could-disappear.html.
42 Mengpin Ge, Johannes Friedrich, and Thomas Damassa, "6 Graphs Explain the World's Top 10 Emitters," World Resources Institute, November 25, 2014, http://www.wri.org/blog/2014/11/6-graphs-explain-world's-top-10-emitters.
43 "Historic Paris Agreement on Climate Change," UN Climate Change Newsroom, last modified December 12, 2015, http://newsroom.unfccc.int/unfccc-newsroom/finale-cop21/.

worst possible consequences of climate change, the world needs to cut greenhouse gas emissions by at least 80 percent below 2005 levels by mid-century.[44] The Paris agreement gets us started along that path, but we will need to continually work to improve upon its goals, both here and around the world. That's why we will work to support more clean energy investment in emerging economies, help developing nations build resilience to the climate impacts we can't avoid, and continue to drive clean energy innovation here at home. And we will continue to work on a bilateral and multilateral basis with our partners, with key countries like China, and with the United Nations climate process to protect our nation, our planet, and our children's future.

As we have described, we will make America the clean-energy superpower of the twenty-first century. We want clean-energy solutions to be invented and developed in America, manufactured in America, and installed and used in America. Not only will that create good-paying jobs here at home, it will demonstrate to the rest of the world the depth of our commitment to combating climate change and altering the way we do business. American leadership is the one force above all others that can prompt other countries to raise their own ambitions. By modeling to the world what the clean-energy future looks like, we will spur more action from China, India, and other major emitters. On top of our investments here at home, we will use our development agencies to help emerging economies "leapfrog" older technologies and embrace clean-energy solutions as they seek to expand access to electricity and modern transportation, in the same way that cellular technology enabled many countries to bypass developing more costly traditional telecommunications infrastructure.

---

44   "FACT SHEET: U.S. Reports its 2025 Emissions Target to the UNFCCC," Press Release, White House, March 31, 2015, https://www.whitehouse.gov/the-press-office/2015/03/31/fact-sheet-us-reports-its-2025-emissions-target-unfccc.

Global health and pandemics.

We face new and novel threats to public health as a result of climate change and globalization. The Zika virus, a mosquito-borne illness that can cause serious birth defects, has spread rapidly in our hemisphere and has infected hundreds of Americans traveling to Central and South America and living in Puerto Rico. Outbreaks of SARS, MERS, and avian influenza have sickened and killed hundreds of people around the world. And the Ebola epidemic in West Africa killed more than 11,000 people.[45]

In the case of Ebola, our global health system proved incapable of quickly and effectively moving to stop the epidemic. U.S. leadership was the single decisive factor in breaking global panic and finally arresting the spread of the epidemic.

Public health is not commonly understood as a security issue, but it should be. Pandemic disease can destabilize regions, undermine economies, and create fertile territory for social and political unrest. Security experts warn that terrorists or hostile nations could use infectious organisms as weapons of war. We need to be clear-eyed about the risks we face and take action to address them.

We need to break the cycle in which our own public health system is beholden to emergency appropriations for specific epidemics, lacking the long-term budget certainty needed to shore up our defenses for the long term, accelerate development of vaccines and new treatments, and keep our people safe. Although hundreds of Americans have been sickened by Zika while abroad, and the mosquitoes that carry the disease have a large footprint in the United States, Congress has repeatedly refused to take action to address the epidemic.

We will create a comprehensive global health strategy that moves beyond the disease-by-disease emergency model and seeks to build a robust, resilient global public health system capable of quickly responding to pandemics. And we will boost support for research and development of drugs, vaccines, diagnostic tools, and medical equipment needed to respond effectively to health crises.

---

45 James Gallager, "Ebola outbreak: How many people have died?," BBC, October 15, 2014, http://www.bbc.com/news/health-29628481.

All of these areas are in need of improvement. In the Ebola epidemic, for instance, the protective suits worn by medical personnel could take as much as an hour to put on and take off, and handling each piece increased the risk of infection. What's more, the suits were sweltering in the West African heat and humidity. As the epidemic went on, USAID launched a Grand Challenge to redesign the suit and reduce the number of steps it takes to don and doff.[46] The Ebola suit illustrates why advances in medical equipment, in addition to developing new drugs and vaccines, will be essential to effectively combating pandemics in the future.

We will also seek permanent structural reform within the World Health Organization, the United Nations, and other vital international organizations. Global health emergencies demand an all-hands-on-deck response, not bureaucratic infighting and delays. And we will work to expand capacity within emerging economies to protect public health, track cases of disease, and rapidly scale emergency medical treatment.

---

46 "Johns Hopkins, DuPont join forces to produce improved Ebola protection suit," Johns Hopkins University, last modified September 28, 2015, http://hub.jhu.edu/2015/09/28/hopkins-dupont-ebola-garment-partnership/.

Nuclear proliferation

The threat of global nuclear proliferation remains one of the greatest security challenges we face. And the threat of nuclear weapons or materials getting into the hands of terrorists is unthinkable. We must intensify our efforts to safeguard nuclear material and work with our allies to block nuclear proliferation, not expand it. We need to ensure that no terrorist is ever able to threaten our country or our allies with a weapon of mass destruction.

To do this, we must first protect nuclear materials and weapons against theft. We've led global efforts to improve nuclear security since the 1990s, but it's time to step up our game. We should continue to invest in our own security here at home, employing new technologies and improving coordination among federal, state, and local authorities. And we must work with our allies and partners in nonproliferation to prevent the smuggling of nuclear materials using improved export controls, intelligence sharing, and border security systems.

Next, we need to reduce the amount of nuclear material worldwide. This includes negotiating a global ban on producing additional materials for nuclear weapons, and working with other countries to minimize the use of weapons-grade material for civil nuclear programs. The new nonproliferation treaty with Russia is a good first step, but we need to continue to strengthen the international framework that prevents proliferation. We must ensure that international treaties, organizations, and institutions like the IAEA have the resources and support they need to do the critical job of monitoring nuclear activity around the world. And we must continue to distrust and verify to guarantee that Iran never acquires a nuclear weapon.

Finally, we need to make very clear that any nation or group that supports or enables terrorist efforts to obtain or use weapons of mass destruction will be held accountable. We will be prepared to use direct military action if that's the only way to prevent terrorists from acquiring or using these weapons.

Cybersecurity

Cyberattacks have profound consequences for our economy and our national security, and offensive advances by nation-states that we know are very technically sophisticated—namely Russia, China, next-level Iran, next-level North Korea—are only going to grow more frequent. We need a comprehensive approach to strengthening cybersecurity that includes working with the private sector to make sure every institution is protected, and improving technology across government, both so workers can better do their jobs and to better protect systems against attacks from both state and non-state actors.

First, our electric grid is increasingly vulnerable to cyberattack.[47] We will modernize North American energy infrastructure to enhance grid security by creating a threat assessment and response team. The purpose of this team would be to improve coordination across federal agencies and strengthen collaboration between state and local officials and the electric power industry to assess and address cybersecurity threats. At the same time, we also need to provide new tools and resources to states, cities, and rural communities to make the investments necessary to improve grid resilience to both cyberattack and extreme weather events.

Second, we must continue to enforce existing sanctions—and impose additional sanctions as needed—on countries like Iran that carry out illicit behaviors like cyberattacks. We have to build on the U.S. Cybersecurity National Action Plan by empowering a federal Chief Information Security Officer and upgrading government-wide cybersecurity.

Third, we also have to navigate the security and civil liberties concerns surrounding the encryption of mobile devices and communications. Impenetrable encryption provides significant cybersecurity advantages, but may also make it harder for law enforcement and counterterrorism professionals to investigate plots and prevent future attacks. Equally, there are legitimate worries about privacy, network security, and creating new vulnerabilities that bad actors—including terrorists—can exploit.

---

47   Shane Harris, "U.S. Electrical Grid Vulnerable to Cyberthreats and Physical Attack, Study Finds," Foreign Policy.com, July 15, 2014, http://foreignpolicy.com/2014/07/15/u-s-electrical-grid-vulnerable-to-cyberthreats-and-physical-attack-study-finds/.

The tech community and the government have to stop seeing each other as adversaries and start working together to protect our safety and our privacy. Creating a National Commission on Encryption could help. And our security professionals could use the advice and talents of technology professionals to help us figure out how to stay ahead of the terrorists. We should reject the false choice between individual privacy and keeping Americans safe by advocating for a strong, balanced approach that leaves each of us secure, our economic innovation protected, and our critical systems resilient.

Stay true to the values that have always made America great.

We are strongest when we lead by our values. They are a key element of our power. And they are what make many societies around the world look to America for leadership. Our commitment to democratic principles and human rights—to promoting more inclusive societies that empower their people—is a core element of who we are and what we stand for. Doing so makes us all safer, more stable, and more prosperous.

We must continue to stand for human rights, for democratic values, and for freedom of speech, religion, and the press worldwide. We must encourage other countries to empower their women and girls because in communities where women thrive, societies thrive. And we have to ensure governments respect equal rights no matter who you are or who you love and hold them accountable when they do not. We need to stand for a single Internet where all of humanity has equal access to knowledge and ideas.

And we must model our values to the world. That means the United States will not commit torture, which insults our democracy, undermines our credibility, and endangers our security. And it means we will at last close the detention facility in Guantánamo Bay, Cuba, which does not keep us safe and provides a potent recruiting tool for terrorists.

We will never, ever stop trying to make our country and world a better place:

- **Promoting women's rights around the globe.** Human rights are women's rights and women's rights are human rights. But in far too many parts of the world, women are still held back. In 2014, one in every four girls was married before the age of eighteen, and laws in 100 economies still restrict the type of work women can do. These laws hold societies back.[48,49]

  Promoting women's rights around the globe has become a cornerstone of U.S. foreign policy. We now have a permanent Ambassador-at-Large for Global Women's Issues, and we've launched the first U.S. strategy to prevent and respond to gender-based violence globally. But there's more to do. Promoting gender equality around the world—from ensuring that girls have equal access to education, to making women safe from sexual violence, to promoting equal economic opportunity—will lead to a more just, secure, and prosperous global community.

- **Fighting for an open Internet abroad.** Technology is a powerful tool for helping solve problems and promoting America's ideals and values around the world. The fundamental rights we cherish—the right to assemble, speak, innovate, and advocate—apply online as well. Civil society across the globe should have the ability to use technology to hold their governments accountable, document abuses, and empower marginalized groups. It is the responsibility of all nations to respect free speech and human rights online. Unfortunately, some countries continue to erect barriers to prevent their people from using the Internet fully and freely. We are in a

---

48 "Ending Child Marriage," UNICEF, http://data.unicef.org/corecode/uploads/document6/uploaded_pdfs/core code/Child-Marriage-Brochure-HR_164.pdf.
49 "Despite Progress, Laws Restricting Economic Opportunity for Women are Widespread Globally, says WBG Report," World Bank, last modified September 9, 2015, http://www.worldbank.org/en/news/press-release/2015/09/09/despite-progress-laws-restricting-economic-opportunity-for-women-are-widespread-globally-says-wbg-report.

contest between the values of open and closed societies, and we must stand with like-minded countries against efforts by countries like China or Russia to block or degrade Internet access, shut down social media, and create a balkanized Internet run by governments. We must also make the business case for the freedom to connect by tying it to the advantages of an expanding global network.

- **Promoting human rights of LGBT people around the world.** Fighting for our values around the world is the right thing to do, and the smart thing to do. While rights for LGBT people are seeing remarkable progress in some parts of the world, including in the United States, the climate for LGBT people in other parts of the world continues to deteriorate. It's a terrible irony: In some parts of the world, life for LGBT people is better than ever; in others, it has never been worse. Hundreds of millions of people live in places where they can be arrested, even executed, for their sexuality or gender identity. And most continue to be discriminated against no matter where they live.

  Promoting LGBT rights has been a key part of this administration's human rights and foreign policy. Thanks to its efforts, the UN has passed two resolutions to protect the LGBT community abroad.[50] But we must continue to apply pressure on other countries to be responsible global stakeholders and live up to their human rights obligations. We must let them know the world is watching. We must increase our investment in the Global Equality Fund, which is committed to empowering LGBT persons to live freely and exercise their rights without fear of discrimination or abuse.[51] And we must ensure that LGBT persons living around the world know that they have an ally in the United States of America.

---

50 "United Nations Resolutions—Sexual orientation and gender identity," United Nations Office of the High Commissioner on Human Rights, 2016, http://www.ohchr.org/EN/Issues/Discrimination/Pages/LGBTUNResolutions.aspx.
51 "Global Equality Fund," U.S. Department of State, 2016, http://www.state.gov/globalequality/.

- **Increasing the number of people on HIV treatment worldwide.**
  The AIDS crisis looks very different today. There are more options for treatment and prevention than ever before. More people
  with HIV are leading full and happy lives. But HIV and AIDS are
  still with us. In sub-Saharan Africa, about 60 percent of new HIV
  infections are in women and girls.[52] Even though the tools exist
  to end this epidemic once and for all, there are still far too many
  people dying today. And that is absolutely inexcusable.

  We must do more together. We must increase global funding for
  HIV and AIDS treatment and prevention. And let's continue
  to increase HIV and AIDS research and invest in the promising innovations and medications that research is producing.
  Programs like PEPFAR have made a significant impact on our
  fight against HIV and AIDS. These efforts have created the
  framework for progress and enjoyed bipartisan support here at
  home and broad support around the world. For the first time,
  an AIDS-free generation is in sight. We must not let up until we
  reach that goal.

- **Embracing development as a tool of American power.** We
  must embrace all the tools of American power, especially development, to be on the front lines of solving tremendous global
  challenges. Investing in development is not only the right thing
  to do, but also the smart thing to do. These investments can
  stabilize developing regions, which in turn keeps our country
  safer and more secure.

  We must target investments to work more deeply in key
  regions, such as improving food security and clean electricity
  in Africa, and addressing corruption and violence in Latin
  America. We should also target states like Yemen and Jordan
  to build jobs, hope, and economic security for those impact-

---

52   "Facts and Figures: HIV and AIDS," United Nations Women, 2015, http://www.unwomen.org/en/what-we-do/
hiv-and-aids/facts-and-figures.

ed by the Syrian crisis, giving them an alternative to violent extremism. And we must prioritize smart aid that engages the private sector to create innovative, efficient solutions to the challenges we face.

- **Ending modern-day slavery.** More than 20 million men, women, and children are trapped in modern slavery.[53] It happens just about everywhere on Earth—including in big cities and small towns across America. Slavery is still part of our lives, our economy, and our communities. Ending modern slavery is one of the great challenges of our time. And it can't be done without American leadership. It also can't be done by America alone. We have to partner with governments, businesses, civil society, faith communities, universities, student groups, and so many others. That's the only way this problem gets solved.

We must concentrate on doing three things. First, we must put survivors at the center. This means devoting more time, energy, and dollars to health and legal services, shelter beds, and job training. And it means increasing our support to the most vulnerable, including children, migrants, runaway kids, and LGBT youth. Second, we must strengthen our government's response and resources. This includes stepping up efforts to prevent and deter human trafficking here at home, increasing law enforcement and transportation security official training so they can spot the signs of trafficking, and data sharing to ensure we are all on the same page in the anti-trafficking fight. And third, we must launch a global alliance. Modern slavery is a global problem, so we need a global solution. We must call on every country on the planet to join together in an alliance to end

---

53 "Forced labour, human trafficking and slavery," International Labour Organization, 2016, http://www.ilo.org/global/topics/forced-labour/lang--en/index.htm.

modern slavery. That means committing to certain policies and programs, tailored to each country and region, based on best practices and rigorous analysis.

Together, we can go a long way toward ending modern slavery. But it will take all of us. And it starts with leadership at the top.

3.

STANDING TOGETHER

Building Bridges, Not Walls

Start of a three-day bus tour—Harrisburg, Pennsylvania, July 29, 2016.

ON JUNE 16, 1858, ABRAHAM LINCOLN began his campaign for the U.S. Senate by giving a speech addressing the evils of slavery. Some thought he lost that Senate race because of that speech. But then he won the Presidency, and some thought it was because of that speech. Lincoln's words are still resonant. "A house divided against itself cannot stand," he declared. "I do not expect the house to fall. But I do expect it will cease to be divided. It will become all one thing or all the other."

While our challenges pale in comparison to Lincoln's, across our country Americans are asking hard questions about whether we are still a house divided. We have staggeringly high levels of income and wealth inequality, despite being the richest country on Earth.[1] The voices of the American people are being drowned out by money and special interests, and it is becoming harder for people to exercise their fundamental right to vote. Our broken immigration system is tearing hardworking families apart. And despite our best efforts and highest hopes, America's long struggle with racism is far from finished.

---

1   Erik Sherman, "America is the richest, and most unequal, country," *Fortune,* September 30, 2015, http://fortune .com/2015/09/30/america-wealth-inequality/.

Too many Americans are still not able to share in the full promise of our country. We need to face that reality—and we need to fix it.

All of this means that the bonds that hold us together as local communities across cities and towns—and as one national community with people of all backgrounds and faiths—have been strained. We have to reclaim the promise of America for everyone, no matter who they vote for. This is not a time for party politics. It's time for all of us to pull together. It's time for us to declare that cooperation is better than conflict, unity is better than division, empowerment is better than resentment— and bridges are better than walls.

To do that, we need to listen to each other. We need to listen to the millions of people crying out for criminal justice reform; to the police officers across the country working hard to keep our communities safe; to the American children of undocumented immigrants scared that one day they'll return from school and their parents will be gone; to the parents from all walks of life passionately calling for relief from gun violence; and to so many others across our nation who are hurting but feel like no one is listening or even cares.

Every family and every community in America should know: You're not on your own. We hear you. We see you. And we will do everything we can to help you.

We need to imagine what it's like to walk in each other's shoes. We need to begin to understand what it's like to be a young black man or a Muslim American or a first-generation Latino American or a police officer. We need to understand the sense of alienation that many working people are feeling, from coal country to our small towns, the sense that they aren't going to be able to give their kids the future they want for them. Finding solutions challenges us to dig deep and constantly seek the right balance. But our country succeeds when all of us share in the promise of America—no matter who you are, what you look like, where you come from, or who you love. There's enough prosperity for everybody.

In 2016, let's take on each other's struggles as our own. Let's fight to break down the barriers that are holding all Americans back. We owe it to our kids, to ourselves, and to our country.

Together, we'll end the era of mass incarceration and replace the school-to-prison pipeline with a cradle-to-college or -career pipeline. We'll make clear, once and for all, that weapons of war have no place on our streets. We'll get secret, unaccountable money out of our politics and make it easier, not harder, to vote. We'll pass comprehensive immigration reform including a path to full and equal citizenship so the 11 million undocumented immigrants contributing to our country can come out of the shadows.[2] We'll make sure that every child receives a quality education, no matter their zip code.

These are just a few of the fights we have to wage—and they won't be easy. We'll have serious disagreements and we'll be up against some pretty powerful forces on the other side. But discussing, debating, arguing, and then pulling together is an idea that goes back to the founding of America, when thirteen separate colonies found a way despite their differences to unite as a single nation. What was true for those early patriots remains true today: We're stronger together. If we have the hard conversations we need to have—and do the hard listening we need to do—we will become an even stronger nation, like steel tempered by fire.

We will provide every child the opportunity to live up to his or her potential, fix our broken immigration system and keep families together, rebalance our criminal justice system, end the epidemic of gun violence, break down the barriers that stand in the way of equal rights, protect voting rights and expand access to the ballot box, and protect our environment and natural resources.

---

2   Jie Zong and Jeanne Batalova, "Frequently Requested Statistics on Immigrants and Immigration in the United States," Migration Policy Institute, May 26, 2016, http://www.migrationpolicy.org/article/frequently-requested-statistics-immigrants-and-immigration-united-states.

**Provide every child the opportunity
to live up to his or her potential.**

—

**Fix our broken immigration system
and keep families together.**

—

Reform our criminal justice system.

—

End the epidemic of gun violence.

—

**Break down the barriers that stand
in the way of equal rights.**

—

**Protect our environment
and natural resources.**

Provide every child the opportunity to live up to his or her potential.

We're a better, stronger, more prosperous country when we harness the talent, hard work, and ingenuity of every single American. To do that, we need to make sure every child in America is able to live up to his or her God-given potential. An African American child should have the same opportunities as a white child. Our cities should do as well as our suburbs. Children living with autism or other disabilities and their families should get the support they need. We don't have a person to waste. Parents across the country desperately want to give their kids a good life and they need help to deal with various pressures. Every child in this country deserves a good teacher, in a good school—regardless of the zip code that child lives in.

Our plan to strengthen public education comes down to TLC: teaching, learning, and community.

America is asking more of our educators than ever before. We look to them to fill in gaps that we as a country have neglected—like helping low-income kids, English-language learners, and kids with disabilities thrive. And we ask them to help right wrongs—from poverty and homelessness to the legacy of racial inequities stretching back centuries. We ask so much of our teachers—and we don't give them enough in return. That's why we will launch a national campaign to modernize and elevate the profession of teaching, and ensure that all educators at every stage of their careers will be able to keep learning, improving, innovating, and earning a living wage—not taking second and third jobs just to make ends meet.

We need to educate our children for the future, not the past. We want our children to be creators, innovators, and entrepreneurs—critical thinkers who can collaborate and communicate within their communities and around the world. That means we need to be reaching for new heights—not rehashing old arguments. When schools get it right, we should replicate their best practices across America, whether they're traditional public schools, community schools, or public charter schools. But we're not going to let people outside the education system foist for-profit schools on our kids. We're not going to accept vouchers that drain resources from public schools. And we need to work together to find the right balance on testing—which can provide critical information to teachers and parents and help kids improve, but only when it doesn't come at the expense of classroom instruction.

And we need more community schools—and more partnerships between schools, social services, and nonprofit organizations to offer a range of support and opportunities for kids. Too many of our public school students are living in poverty. Too many students go to school hungry or exhausted from a long night at a shelter. They have the weight of the world on their little shoulders. We need to tackle all the problems holding our kids back—and we need to do it together. Kids shouldn't have to be from a wealthy family to join a soccer team or have access to mental health services. These services and opportunities should be within reach for all our kids.

We know that our next generation is our most precious asset. That's why we have a plan to support children throughout their education, starting with early education. We will ensure every four-year-old has access to high-quality preschool. We also have to support parents by curbing childcare costs and awarding scholarships to student-parents so they can focus on their families and their education. We will nurture our kids as they get older by building a strong public education system.

We believe the quality of our public education system for this generation of students will affect our country and our economy for years to come. Getting the economy moving goes hand in hand with education. We can't get good jobs with rising incomes unless we have a good public education system. Part of a world-class public education system will be making sure students with disabilities are supported. We have to take care of the Americans who are too young to vote. It is essential that we set our kids and our country up for success.

That's why we will:

- Expand early childhood education to provide our kids a strong start
- Guarantee a world-class K–12 education for every child in every community
- Support the millions of Americans with autism and their families

Expand early childhood education to provide
our kids a strong start.

We know early development is critical for children—new research shows early learning in the first five years of life can have a significant impact on lifelong education. But just half of the roughly 8.1 million three- and four-year-olds in the United States are enrolled in pre-K,[3] and only one in four are enrolled in publicly funded pre-K.[4] Nationwide, state funding for pre-K programs increased by $479 million in just one year—an 8.3 percent increase in state investment.[5] There is bipartisan agreement on the need to invest in preschool. The states that funded pre-K programs had Republican and Democratic governors.[6] But federal funding has not followed.[7]

That's why we will:

- **Make preschool universal for every four-year-old in America.** Expanding access to high-quality preschool for children helps strengthen families and communities, and gives children a hand up to opportunity later in life. We will ensure that every four-year-old in this country has access to high-quality preschool in the next ten years. The evidence is clear that universal preschool will help reduce inequality over the long term, improve school performance, and allow parents to rest easier knowing their kids are learning and cared for.[8]

- **Significantly increase childcare investments so that no family in America has to pay more than 10 percent of its income to afford high-quality childcare.** The cost of childcare has

---

3 "School Enrollment: CPS October 2013—Detailed Tables," United States Census Bureau, https://www.census.gov/hhes/school/data/cps/2013/tables.html.
4 "School Enrollment: CPS October," United States Census Bureau.
5 Bruce Atchison and Emily Workman, "State Pre-K Funding: 2014-15 fiscal year," Education Commission of the States, January 2015, http://www.ecs.org/clearinghouse/01/16/97/11697.pdf.
6 Ibid.
7 Ibid.
8 Ibid.

increased by nearly 25 percent during the past decade, while the wages of working families have stagnated.[9] These high costs severely squeeze working families, prevent too many children from getting a healthy start, and act as a disincentive for parents to stay in the workforce. We will fight for every family in America to have access to high-quality, affordable childcare by significantly increasing the federal government's investment in childcare subsidies and providing tax relief for the cost of child care to working families.

- **Double our investment in high-quality early learning programs.** Early Head Start provides comprehensive services to our youngest learners and their families—including health, nutrition, and pre-literacy support with a strong focus on children's social and emotional development. The Early Head Start-Child Care Partnership program brings Early Head Start's evidence-based curriculum into the childcare setting to provide comprehensive, full-day, high-quality services to low-income families. To ensure our children have a strong foundation to learn, and to provide critical support to working families, we will double the number of children served by Early Head Start and the Early Head Start-Child Care Partnership program. And we will support proven programs like HIPPY that empower parents to become their children's first teachers.

- **Expand access to evidence-based home visiting programs.** There is increasing scientific evidence that brain development in the earliest years of childhood is crucial to economic success[10] The first three years are particularly important. Eighty percent of the brain is formed and vital foundations for vocabulary are established by the age of three. That's why we

---

9   Elise Gould, "Why America's Workers Need Faster Wage Growth—And What We Can Do About It," Economic Policy Institute, August 27, 2014, http://www.epi.org/publication/why-americas-workers-need-faster-wage-growth/.
10   Karen Bogenschneider and Olivia Little, eds., "The Science of Early Brain Development: A Foundation for the Success of Our Children and the State Economy," Purdue University, January 22, 2014, https://www.purdue.edu/hhs/hdfs/fii/wp-content/uploads/2015/07/s_wifis32report.pdf.

will double our investment in evidenced-based home visiting programs such as the Maternal, Infant and Early Childhood Home Visiting program. These programs—which provide home visits by a social worker or nurse during and directly after pregnancy—significantly improve maternal and child health, development, and learning. And we will also do more to support proven programs that do not require direct intervention from nurses or social workers, like the HIPPY program.

**Guarantee a world-class K–12 education
for every child in every community.**

We believe that every child in this country deserves a good teacher in a good school regardless of the zip code you live in. Just like our kids, our education system needs TLC: support for teachers, support for learning, and support for communities. That means supporting parents to be their child's first teachers and expanding access to high-quality childcare and universal preschool. It means supporting our teachers, not scapegoating them. It means repairing our crumbling schools and investing in training and support for our educators. Because when we invest in education, we're investing in our country's future, and a stronger economy for all of us.

That's why we will:

- **Launch a national campaign to modernize and elevate the profession of teaching.** America is asking more of our educators than ever before. That's why we will launch a national campaign to elevate and modernize the teaching profession by preparing, supporting, and paying every child's teacher as if the future of our country is in their hands—because it is. We also need to be serious about raising wages for teachers and support staff.

  And the last thing a teacher needs when they are just starting out is a mountain of student debt. We will fight to ensure future students don't have to borrow a dime to attend public colleges or universities. For families making less than $125,000 a year, we'll eliminate tuition at public colleges and universities altogether. And for the millions who already have student debt, you'll be able to refinance your student loans, so you never have to pay more than you can afford. For people who go into public service—including teaching—any remaining debt will be forgiven after ten years. We also need to be serious about raising wages for teachers. Anyone who works full-time in America should be able to earn a living wage, without taking second and third jobs just to get by.

- **Expect great schools.** It's time to stop focusing only on "failing schools." Let's focus on our great schools so we can build on their success. When schools get it right, we should share their best practices across America, whether they're traditional public schools, community schools, or public charter schools that serve every student.

- **Close the education achievement gap.** We have to close the gap for low-income students, students of color, English-language learners, and students with disabilities. Right now, our education system is failing too many children. Our schools are more segregated than they were in 1968, and there's still a big achievement gap between white students and their black and Latino peers.[11] We will double America's investment in Early Head Start, ensure that every four-year-old in America has access to high-quality preschool, drive student achievement in K–12 schools, make college affordable, and relieve the crushing burden of student debt.

---

11 Gary Orfield, Erica Frankenberg, et al., eds, "Brown at 60: Great Progress, a Long Retreat and an Uncertain Future," The Civil Rights Project, May 15, 2014, https://civilrightsproject.ucla.edu/research/k-12-education/integration-and-diversity/brown-at-60-great-progress-a-long-retreat-and-an-uncertain-future/Brown-at-60-051814.pdf.

Percentage of students at or above proficiency for their grade level

■ White   ■ Black   ■ Hispanic

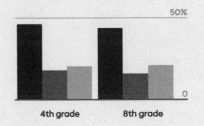

Reading

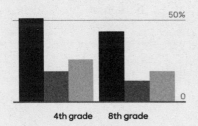

Math

- **Support communities.** The challenges a student faces outside of school walls often carry over into the classroom. It's hard for a young child to focus in class if he is hungry, or if she doesn't know where her family is sleeping that night. Students in communities affected by gun violence are often traumatized. Too often we make our public schools responsible for solving broader social problems without providing specialized resources or support for wrap-around services. We will do more to support partnerships between schools, social services, and high-quality nonprofit organizations to build stronger schools and stronger communities, and to offer the support and opportunities our kids need to succeed in school and in life.

- **Provide every student in America an opportunity to learn computer science.** We need to educate our children for the future, not the past. We want our children to be creators, innovators, and entrepreneurs—critical thinkers who can collaborate and communicate within their own communities and around the world. There are more than half a million open jobs that require computing skills—across the country and in every major industry.[12] But the majority of schools in the United States don't offer computer science.[13] We will provide states and school districts funding to help scale computer science instruction and lesson programs that improve student achievement or increase college enrollment and completion in computer science education fields.

---

12   "TechHire Initiative," The White House, accessed July 2016, https://www.whitehouse.gov/issues/technology/techhire.
13   Adams Nager and Robert D. Atkinson, "The Case for Improving U.S. Computer Science Education," Information Technology & Innovation Foundation, May 31, 2016, https://itif.org/publications/2016/05/31/case-improving-us-computer-science-education.

Support the millions of Americans
with autism and their families.

More than 3.5 million Americans are believed to have autism spectrum disorder, including an estimated one in every sixty-eight children.[14] And the cost of treatment and services is more than most families can afford.[15] Improving support for children and adults with autism can vastly improve their lives and make the cost more sustainable for families as well as for Medicaid and other public programs.

We have a plan to support these Americans and their families. We will launch a nationwide campaign to diagnose autism early. We will expand insurance coverage for autism services so that every family can afford the support they need. We will protect students with autism from abuse in schools, and open up employment opportunities for them after they graduate. We also have to invest in more research to deepen our understanding of autism. And we will provide support to caregivers of people with autism.

We believe that our country must make supporting individuals and families with autism a priority—for the millions of people living with autism and their loved ones, and millions more who will be diagnosed in the future.

---

14 "Facts and Statistics," Autism Society, last modified August 25, 2015, accessed July 2016, http://www.autism-society.org/what-is/facts-and-statistics/.
15 "Lifetime Costs of Autism Average $1.4 Million to $2.4 Million," Autism Speaks, June 9, 2014, https://www.autismspeaks.org/science/science-news/lifetime-costs-autism-average-millions.

That's why we will:

- **Conduct a nationwide early screening outreach campaign.**
  Children as young as two years old can show signs of autism,
  but many aren't diagnosed until months or even years later.[16]
  Studies suggest that children who are African American, Latino,
  or female are especially likely to be diagnosed too late.[17,18,19] Our
  plan would help ensure that all children, and in particular children
  from underserved backgrounds, can get screened for autism.

- **Expand insurance coverage for autism services.** When autism
  services aren't covered by insurance, they are unaffordable for
  many families. We will push states to require health insurance
  coverage for autism services—both behavioral and developmental—in private insurance plans and those offered through the
  Affordable Care Act marketplace.

- **Invest in more research to deepen our understanding of
  autism.** We need more research to better understand child
  brain development and the genetic linkages for autism, create
  better diagnostic tools, and improve treatments and services for
  people on the autism spectrum and their families at every stage
  of life. We will significantly increase government investment
  in autism-related research, from studies that improve patient
  services to research that identifies more genetic markers. We
  will also call for the first-ever study on the prevalence of adults
  on the autism spectrum.

---

16 "Facts About ASD," Centers for Disease Control and Prevention, accessed July 28, 2016, http://www.cdc.gov/ncbddd/autism/facts.html.
17 "Regressive Autism Reported Twice as Often among African American Children," Autism Speaks, May 6, 2014, https://www.autismspeaks.org/science/science-news/regressive-autism-reported-twice-often-among-african-american-children.
18 Katherine E. Zuckerman et al., "Latino Parents' Perspectives of Barriers to Autism Diagnosis," National Center for Biotechnology Information, 2014, http://www.ncbi.nlm.nih.gov/pmc/articles/PMC4006363/.
19 Maia Szalavitz, "Autism—It's Different in Girls," *Scientific American,* March 1, 2016, http://www.scientificamerican.com/article/autism-it-s-different-in-girls/.

- **Increase employment opportunities for individuals with autism.** Fewer than half of all youth with autism are employed or pursuing higher education in the two years after they graduate from high school.[20] We will launch the Autism Works Initiative to increase resources and establish public-private partnerships to help students with autism after they graduate connect with adults with autism to find new employment opportunities.

- **Keep students with autism safe at school.** Students with autism are particularly vulnerable to bullying, abuse, and injury at school.[21] We will enact the Keeping All Students Safe Act and other reforms to protect children with autism from abuse in their schools. We will also toughen the U.S. Department of Education guidance on bullying to protect children with autism from harassment.

- **Provide new support to caregivers.** We will provide new funds through the Developmental Disabilities Act to expand support for family members and other caregivers providing long-term care for those with autism and other disabilities. We will build on the robust agenda to help those in the caring economy that we previously outlined by expanding support for families and caregivers of individuals with developmental disabilities.

---

20   Anne M. Roux et al., "National Autism Indicators Report: Transition into Young Adulthood," http://drexel
.edu/autisminstitute/research-projects/research/ResearchPrograminLifeCourseOutcomes/indicatorsreport/#st-
hash.31XId4lN.crKnUVkn.dpuf.
21   "New Data Show Children with Autism Bullied Three Times More Frequently than Their Unaffected Siblings,"
Kennedy Krieger Institute, March 26, 2012, https://www.kennedykrieger.org/overview/news/new-data-show-children-
autism-bullied-three-times-more-frequently-their-unaffected-siblings.

Fix our broken immigration system and keep families together.

America was built by immigrants. Our economy depends on immigrants. Our future will be written, in part, by immigrants. No matter how long ago our ancestors arrived in this land, whether they came by foot or boat or plane, across the Pacific, the Atlantic, or the Rio Grande, all of us owe a debt of gratitude to the immigrants who helped make America the greatest country in the world.

But today in America our immigration system is badly broken. Millions of immigrants are living and working in the shadows, many continuing to earn lower wages and lag behind in educational attainment. And while America's immigrants have become an integral part of our country's social fabric, many live in fear that deportation will tear their families apart.

We are a bighearted country where people of all races, religions, and nationalities can find a home. Our immigration system should live up to those values. Our immigration system should prioritize families and protect those fleeing persecution. It should attract innovators and entrepreneurs to start businesses and create jobs in America. And it should keep our country secure by focusing our enforcement resources on those who pose a threat to public safety, not law-abiding immigrant families contributing to their communities.

Cheska is a DREAMer. She came to the United States from the Philippines with her family when she was a young girl. Her father had a work visa, but he lost his job in the recession—and the whole family became undocumented. When Cheska was a senior in high school, with teachers asking her every day about her college plans, she found the courage to tell her ROTC instructor about her status. Her school stepped up, supported her, helped her investigate the Deferred Action for Childhood Arrivals program and apply for relief from deportation.

That is America at its best. Now, we need to make sure that Cheska and other DREAMers like her have every chance to build the lives they want in the country they call home. Not only because it's right, but also because we are stronger when we do. When we embrace immigrants, not denigrate them. When we build bridges, not walls.

That's why we will:

- Fight for comprehensive immigration reform
- Keep immigrant families together
- Support immigrant integration

Fight for comprehensive immigration reform.

America has always been a place where people from around the world can come to pursue their dreams, start new businesses, and apply their talents to American growth and innovation. But for too long our broken immigration system has kept would-be Americans from fully participating in our country—or from coming here at all. It's time for that to change.

There is a greater consensus than ever before that we must work together to reform our immigration system. We will turn that consensus into action and introduce comprehensive immigration reform legislation within our first one hundred days in office. That means addressing all aspects of the system, including immigrants living here today and those who wish to come in the future, from highly skilled workers to family members to those seeking refuge from violence and persecution.

There is a greater consensus than ever before that we must work together to reform our immigration system. We will turn that consensus into action and introduce comprehensive immigration reform legislation within our first one hundred days in office.

To immigrant families this is an issue that matters more than we can measure. That's why we will fight for comprehensive immigration reform that offers a path to full and equal citizenship. If you work hard, love this country, and contribute your talents, you deserve a chance to come forward and become a citizen. Comprehensive immigration reform will provide immigrants a chance to come out of the shadows and into the formal economy. It will encourage foreign students to conduct research and foreign entrepreneurs to start businesses in America. And it will add $800 billion to our gross domestic product, creating new jobs for all Americans and more growth for our economy.

We should never forget that this debate is about people who work hard, who love this country, who pay taxes to it, and want nothing more than to build a good future for themselves and their children. That's why comprehensive immigration reform must put families first and fix the family visa backlog. Backlogs in our current immigration system are preventing family members of lawful permanent residents and American citizens from securing visas. Applicants from Asian countries make up some 40 percent of the backlog, and some applicants from the Philippines have been waiting for a visa for as long as twenty-three years.[22] We will reduce the backlog to reunite families in a timelier manner and reduce the pressure on family members to migrate illegally.

Finally, comprehensive reform will keep our communities safer. It will give law enforcement the resources they need to strengthen our borders, focus on crime and criminals, and harness technology to address threats to our national security.

If we believe we are an American family, then we need to pull together and solve the outstanding issues around our broken immigration system. Americans across the political spectrum support reform, from labor unions to the U.S. Chamber of Commerce, not just because it's the right thing to do—and it is—but because they know it strengthens families, our economy, and our country.[23]

We can't wait any longer. We will keep pushing Congress to act and keep raising the stakes until we pass the comprehensive immigration reform our families need.

22 Esther Yu-His Lee, "It's Much Harder To Immigrate To The U.S. Than It Is To Buy A Gun," ThinkProgress, June 14, 2016, http://thinkprogress.org/immigration/2016/06/14/3788051/harder-to-come-to-us-than-to-buy-gun/.
23 Kevin Bogardus, "Chamber, union leaders mull alliance to press for immigration reform," *The Hill*, January 16, 2013, http://thehill.com/business-a-lobbying/277397-chamber-unions-mull-immigration-alliance.

Keep immigrant families together.

As we fight for comprehensive immigration reform, we must do everything we can to keep immigrant families together. These are our friends and family members; neighbors and classmates; DREAMers and parents of Americans and lawful permanent residents. Our immigrant families make our nation stronger, smarter, and more creative. They enrich our communities and contribute to our economy every day.

Our immigration system should live up to our values as a country. Children should be able to go to school without worrying that their parents may not be there when they return. They should be able to go to sleep without worrying about being torn away from the only country they've ever known. So while we focus our enforcement resources on those who pose a threat to public safety, we must do everything we can to keep immigrant families together.

This is especially important for little girls like Karla. Karla is a typical eleven-year-old. She loves science experiments, math, and *Ella Enchanted*. But she leaves for school every day terrified that her mom and dad won't be there when she gets home. Her parents had to take her to a heart specialist, who explained that living in constant fear was making her heart beat dangerously fast. We need to reform our broken immigration system so Karla and millions of American kids like her can be just that—kids.

That's why instead of breaking up law-abiding immigrant families who have enriched America, we will do everything possible under the law to protect them. We will:

- **Defend the Deferred Action for Childhood Arrivals (DACA) and Deferred Action for Parental Accountability (DAPA) programs.** More than 16 million people live in mixed-status families, with at least one member not a citizen or lawful permanent resident.[24] Hundreds of thousands of people have ben-

24 Joanna Dreby, "How Today's Immigration Enforcement Policies Impact Children, Families, and Communities: A View from the Ground," Center for American Progress, August 2012, https://www.americanprogress.org/wp-content/uploads/2012/08/DrebyImmigrationFamilies_execsumm.pdf.

efited from DACA already, and an estimated 5 million people are eligible for DAPA.[25] While the Supreme Court's deadlocked decision on DAPA threw millions of families across our country into a state of uncertainty, it is important to remember the decision was purely procedural and casts no doubt on the fact that the President acted entirely within his legal authority. We will do everything we can to defend DACA and DAPA against partisan attacks and politically motivated lawsuits that would put DREAMers and others at risk of deportation.

- **Build on President Obama's executive actions to help others with sympathetic cases be eligible for deferred action.** We will establish a simple, accessible system for other immigrants with sympathetic cases—such as parents of DREAMers, those with a history of service and contribution to their communities, or others who experience extreme labor violations—to make their case and be eligible for deferred action.

- **Repeal the three- and ten-year bars.** The three- and ten-year bars force families—especially those whose members have different citizenship or immigration statuses—into a heartbreaking dilemma: remain in the shadows, or pursue a green card by leaving the country and your loved ones behind.[26] To allow those already eligible for a green card to obtain one without tearing families apart, we will work to repeal the three- and ten-year bars.

---

25 "DACA Has Improved the Lives of Hundreds of Thousands of Undocumented Young People," Generation Progress, November 2014 http://genprogress.org/about/press/2014/11/19/33165/release-daca-has-improved-the-lives-of-hundreds-of-thousands-of-undocumented-young-people; and "Executive Actions on Immigration," Department of Homeland Security, United States Citizenship and Immigration Services, last modified April 15, 2015, accessed July 2016, https://www.uscis.gov/immigrationaction.
26 "So Close and Yet So Far: How the Three- and Ten-Year Bars Keep Families Apart," American Immigration Council, July 25, 2011, http://www.immigrationpolicy.org/just-facts/so-close-and-yet-so-far-how-three-and-ten-year-bars-keep-families-apart.

- **End the raids and roundups, and conduct humane and targeted immigration enforcement.** If we want to have an honest conversation about immigrant families, we must admit this: A lot of children in America say good-bye to their parents every morning afraid that their mom or dad won't be there when they get home. And for too many kids, those fears come true. We believe immigration enforcement must be humane and live up to our American values. We will focus our resources on detaining and deporting those individuals who pose a violent threat to public safety, and work to ensure those who seek asylum have a fair chance to tell their stories.

- **End family detention and close private detention facilities.** We will end family detention for parents and children who arrive at our border in desperate situations. We have alternatives to detention for those who pose no flight or public safety risk, such as supervised release, that have proved effective and cost a fraction of what it takes to keep families in detention.[27] We will also end private immigrant detention centers. We need to move away from contracting out this critical government function to private corporations and private industry incentives that may contribute—or have the appearance of contributing—to over-incarceration.

- **Humanely address the Central American migrant crisis.** Since 2014, tens of thousands of Central American migrants have arrived at our border seeking refuge from violence and economic conditions in their country, and many of these migrants are unaccompanied children.[28] We must address both the root causes of this issue and the circumstances of this population once they arrive in the United States. We will stop the raids that

---

27 "Alternatives to Detention: Improved Data Collection and Analyses Needed to Better Assess Program Effectiveness," United States Government Accountability Office, GAO-15-26, November 2014, http://www.gao.gov/assets/670/666911.pdf.

28 Sibylla Brodzinsky, "US and Mexico agree to improve asylum access for tens of thousands of refugees," *Guardian,* July 12, 2016, https://www.theguardian.com/world/2016/jul/12/us-mexico-asylum-agreement-central-america-refugees.

are happening in these immigrant communities because they cause unnecessary fear and disruption. No mother or child in America should go to sleep at night afraid of hearing a knock on the door and getting ripped out of bed. We will ensure government-funded counsel for all unaccompanied minors in immigration court so that no child has to defend themselves in removal proceedings without an attorney. Finally, we will crack down on criminal organizations, and work with regional partners and invest in sustained economic development to strengthen conditions on the ground in Central America.

Support immigrant integration.

Today, the United States is home to an estimated 42 million immigrants—13 percent of our population. Yet, despite the steady growth of America's immigrant population, immigrants still face significant language, education, and economic barriers that prevent them from fully participating in their new home. We need to break down these barriers and ensure that in America everyone feels welcome and everyone has a fair chance at success.

To do that, we must make sure immigrants are connected to workforce training and are offered the education and language services they need to thrive. We also must do more to help the estimated 9 million lawful permanent residents in the United States who may want to become citizens. It's so powerful—and so precious—to be a citizen of the United States and to have a voice in this nation's future. Let's support those who are eligible and want to accept the privileges and responsibilities of citizenship to take that final step.

To ensure America's immigrants a real chance at success, we will:

- **Create a national Office of Immigrant Affairs to ensure successful immigrant and refugee integration.** Given the cross-cutting nature of immigrant integration policy concerns, it's critical that there be a proactive effort to coordinate policies and programs across federal agencies and with state and local governments. We will create the first ever federal Office of Immigrant Affairs to ensure there is a dedicated place in the White House where integration policies and services for immigrants and refugees are managed.

- **Promote naturalization.** There are an estimated 9 million lawful permanent residents in the United States who are eligible to become U.S. citizens. We need to do more to help them take that last step. We will work to expand fee waivers so more people can get a break on costs, increase access to robust language programs to help people boost their English proficiency, and enhance outreach and education so more people are informed about their options and engaged in the process.

- **Support affordable integration services through $15 million in new grant funding for community navigators and similar organizations.** Immigrant integration starts at the local level where volunteers, community-based organizations, and legal services providers are often the first people to welcome immigrants into their new communities and help them get settled. We will create a new competitive grant program to supplement current funding streams for integration and naturalization services, focusing on building the capacity of organizations in the field. This will ensure that more immigrants can receive the support they need to apply for naturalization or DAPA and DACA, seek out education and workforce training, and navigate their new communities.

- **Significantly increase federal resources for adult English-language education and citizenship education.** English proficiency is essential to social and economic mobility in the United States. But for too many immigrants, accessing affordable and effective English-language learning resources continues to be a struggle. Of the roughly 23 million adults 16 and over in the country who have limited English proficiency, fewer than 1 million benefit from the primary federal-state partnership program for providing adult English instruction. We will greatly expand the federal resources devoted to adult English-language education and citizenship education—ensuring that immigrants, citizenship applicants, parents of young children, and others can access the programs they need, whether at community organizations, public libraries, adult schools, community colleges, or through new innovative platforms.

Reform our criminal justice system.

Our criminal justice system is broken. Only about 5 percent of the world's population lives in the United States, but we are home to about 25 percent of the world's prisoners. We need to support our police officers, who put their lives on the line every day. We also need to address the fact that too many African Americans have lost their lives at the hands of the police. These things go hand in hand. Everyone is safer when there is respect for the law and when everyone is respected by the law.

To successfully reform our criminal justice system, we must bring police and communities together to rebuild the bonds of trust. We must find alternatives to prison for nonviolent offenders, address racial disparities in sentencing and mandatory minimums, and end the era of mass incarceration. And we have to do more to ensure that the hundreds of thousands of people who return to their communities every year from prison get a real second chance.

But we also have to acknowledge that, on their own, policy change won't be enough. On their own, our thoughts and prayers aren't enough, either. Ending the systemic racism that plagues our country—and rebuilding our communities so the police and local communities all see themselves as being on the same side—will require contributions from all of us. White Americans need to do a better job of listening when African Americans talk about the seen and unseen barriers they face every day. We need to try, as best we can, to walk in one another's shoes, to imagine what it would be like if people followed us around stores, or locked their car doors when we walked past.

We also need to put ourselves in the shoes of police officers, kissing their kids and spouses good-bye every day and heading off to do a dangerous job that their families pray will bring them home safe at night. Empathy works both ways. We have to try to see the world through their eyes, too. When you get right down to it, that's what makes it possible for people from every background, every race, every religion, to come together as one nation. It's what makes our country endure.

To make real, lasting change in our communities and reform our criminal justice system, we will:

- Strengthen bonds of trust between communities and police
- Reform our criminal justice system and end the era of mass incarceration
- Help formerly incarcerated people successfully reenter society

Strengthen bonds of trust between communities and police.

In order to build trust in our communities, we must promote effective, accountable, constitutional policing. There continues to be too little trust in too many places between police and the communities they serve. In particular, we need to bring people together to improve trust between police and the African-American community. However, we should also recognize that many police officers and departments across the country are inspiring trust and confidence and deploying creative and effective strategies. We should build on what is working as well as adopt new and needed reforms.

We also need to support law enforcement. In July, five police officers lost their lives in Dallas in a vicious attack targeting police. When they were killed, they were protecting a peaceful protest. For years before that horrible night, the Dallas Police Department had worked to earn a reputation for excellence, to improve policing, and strengthen their bonds with their community.[29] We need to recognize the good work of police departments like Dallas, and to accumulate and disseminate best practices on community policing, use of force, and other vital law enforcement activities.

Dallas isn't alone. Police officers across the country are pouring their hearts into this work because they know it is vital to the peace, tranquillity, justice, and equality of America.

---

29   Radley Balko, "What Dallas's historically low murder rate can teach us about policing," *Washington Post*, January 12, 2015, https://www.washingtonpost.com/news/the-watch/wp/2015/01/12/what-dallass-historically-low-murder-rate-can-teach-us-about-policing/.

That is why we will:

- **Bring law enforcement and communities together to develop national guidelines on the use of force by law enforcement.** We need to make it clear when deadly force is warranted and when it isn't and emphasize proven methods for de-escalating situations.

- **Acknowledge that implicit bias still exists across society—even in the best police departments—and tackle it together.** We will commit $1 billion in our first budget to find and fund the best training programs, support new research, and make this a national policing priority.

- **Make new investments to support state-of-the-art law enforcement training programs at every level.** These programs will focus on issues like use of force, de-escalation, community policing and problem solving, alternatives to incarceration, crisis intervention, and officer safety and wellness.

- **Support legislation to end racial profiling by federal, state, and local law enforcement officials.** Racial profiling does not make our communities safer, and this practice should be ended at all levels of law enforcement.

- **Strengthen the U.S. Department of Justice's pattern or practice unit—the unit that addresses civil rights violations.** We will accomplish this by increasing the department's resources, working to secure subpoena power, and improving data collection for pattern or practice investigations.

- **Double funding for the U.S. Department of Justice's Collaborative Reform program.** Across the country, there are police departments deploying creative and effective strategies that we can learn from and build on. We will provide assistance and training to agencies to apply these best practices.

- **Provide federal matching funds to make body cameras available to every police department in America.** Body cameras increase police accountability and transparency, and provide documentation of interactions between police and civilians. We need more police departments to use this important tool in their work to help rebuild trust with the communities they serve.

- **Promote oversight and accountability in use of controlled equipment.** This includes limiting the transfer of military equipment to local law enforcement from the federal government, eliminating the one-year use requirement, and requiring transparency from agencies that purchase equipment using federal funds.

- **Collect and report national data.** We need better data to inform policing strategies and provide greater transparency and accountability when it comes to crime, officer-involved shootings, and deaths in custody.

Reform our criminal justice system and end the era of mass incarceration.

Although the United States is home to only about 5 percent of the world's population, we have about 25 percent of the total prison population. We incarcerate some 2.3 million people—four times more than in 1980.[30] That means that today in America, more than one out of every 100 adults is behind bars.

The inequities that persist in our justice system undermine the shared vision of what America can be and should be. They also do little to reduce crime. A significant number of those incarcerated in federal, state, and local prisons are nonviolent offenders.

We need to reform our criminal justice system so that nonviolent offenders can be diverted from serving hard time where appropriate, mandatory minimums no longer reinforce and perpetuate racial disparities or result in disproportionate sentences, and the era of mass incarceration can be brought to an end. Our current criminal justice system imposes significant costs on our communities and the government. One in every twenty-eight children now has a parent in prison. African American men are far more likely to be stopped and searched by police, charged with crimes, and sentenced to longer prison terms than white men found guilty of the same offenses.[31,32]

That's why we will:

• **Pursue alternatives to incarceration.** We should work together to pursue alternative punishments for nonviolent offenders where appropriate. We don't want to create another "incarceration generation." We will issue guidance to federal prosecutors on

---

30 "Criminal Justice Fact Sheet," National Association for the Advancement of Colored People, 2016, http://www.naacp.org/pages/criminal-justice-fact-sheet.

31 Ted Miller, Bruce Lawrence, et al., "Perils of Police Action: A Cautionary Tale from U.S. Data Sets," *Injury Prevention Journal,* July 25, 2016, http://injuryprevention.bmj.com/content/early/2016/07/27/injury prev-2016-042023.

32 "Written Submission of the ACLU on Racial Disparities in Sentencing," American Civil Liberties Union, October 27, 2014, https://www.aclu.org/sites/default/files/assets/141027_iachr_racial_disparities_aclu_submission_0.pdf.

prioritizing treatment and rehabilitation, rather than incarceration, for nonviolent offenders.

- **Take action on mandatory minimum sentencing.** Excessive federal mandatory minimum sentences keep nonviolent drug offenders in prison for longer than is necessary or useful and have increased racial inequities in our criminal justice system. We will cut mandatory minimum sentences for drug offenses in half. This will include eliminating the sentencing disparity for crack and powder cocaine so that equal amounts of crack carry the same sentence as powder cocaine, granting additional discretion to judges in applying mandatory minimum sentencing, and reforming the "strike" system to focus on violent crime by narrowing the category of prior offenses that count as strikes to exclude nonviolent drug offenses.

- **Focus federal enforcement resources on violent crime, not simple marijuana possession.** Marijuana arrests, including for simple possession, account for a large number of drug arrests. Significant racial disparities exist in marijuana enforcement, with black men significantly more likely to be arrested for marijuana possession than their white counterparts, even though usage rates are similar.[33] To address these issues, we will allow states that have enacted marijuana laws to act as laboratories of democracy, as long as they adhere to certain federal priorities such as not selling to minors, preventing intoxicated driving, and keeping organized crime out of the industry. We will also reschedule marijuana from a Schedule I to a Schedule II substance to advance research into its health benefits.

- **End the privatization of prisons.** We should move away from contracting out this core responsibility of the federal government to private corporations, and from creating private indus-

---

33 "The War on Marijuana in Black and White," American Civil Liberties Union, June 2013, https://www.aclu.org/report/war-marijuana-black-and-white?redirect=criminal-law-reform/war-marijuana-black-and-white.

try incentives that may contribute—or have the appearance of contributing—to over-incarceration.

- **End the school-to-prison pipeline.** We believe our schools should lead all students toward opportunity and provide them with a sense of hope. Parents, teachers, and students all want safe, welcoming schools, but in some communities—especially African American communities—police involvement in school discipline, an over-reliance on suspensions and expulsions, and implicit biases are leading students into a school-to-prison pipeline.[34] We will disrupt this pipeline by transforming how we approach discipline in schools, providing funding for reform of disciplinary systems, training teachers on classroom climate and restorative justice, and calling on states to eliminate overly broad school disturbance laws.

Even though black students make up only 16 percent of the student population

31 percent of students who are subjected to school-related arrests are black.

---

34   Sarah Redfield and Jason Nance, "School-to-Prison Pipeline: Preliminary Report," American Bar Association, February 2016, http://www.americanbar.org/content/dam/aba/administrative/diversity_pipeline/stp_preliminary_report_final.authcheckdam.pdf.

Help formerly incarcerated people successfully reenter society.

More than 600,000 people annually return to their communities from prison, and millions more come home following time in jail for low-level offenses.[35] Too many returning citizens lack the tools they need to succeed following release—including employment, housing, and continuity of health care, such as addiction and mental health issues. In particular, they often face barriers to being considered for jobs for which they are qualified.

We are a nation of second chances—it's time we start acting like it.

Derreck knows about giving people a second chance. He is the owner of the Home of Chicken and Waffles in Oakland, California, where he almost exclusively employs formerly incarcerated people who are on probation or reentering our society. He gives them an opportunity they probably otherwise would not have to make a fair wage and get back on their feet.

Mikey grew up in New York City public housing, and his life took a turn when he was arrested for marijuana possession with intent to sell. Once released on probation, he had a difficult time getting a fresh start. No one wanted to hire someone who had been incarcerated. So Mikey took it upon himself to start his own business. He began making ice cream out of his apartment, and now runs Mikey Likes It ice cream shop down the street from where he grew up. He uses his success to advocate for people like him, who deserve a second shot at making a better life.

Not only is this an economic issue, it's a family issue, too. More than half of people who are currently incarcerated are parents of minors, and half of children with parents in prison are under age ten.[36] Mass incarceration has an explicit racial bias, as one in three black men can expect to go to prison in their lifetime.[37] We must reform our criminal justice

---

35 "FACT SHEET: State of the Union: Cabinet in Your Community—Department of Justice," Department of Justice Office of Public Affairs, U.S. Department of Justice, January 13, 2016, https://www.justice.gov/opa/pr/fact-sheet-state-union-cabinet-your-community-department-justice.

36 Lauren E. Glaze and Laura M. Maruschak, "Bureau of Justice Statistics Special Report: Parents in Prison and Their Minor Children," U.S. Department of Justice, March 30, 2010, http://www.bjs.gov/content/pub/pdf/pptmc.pdf.

37 Christopher Lyons and Becky Pettit, "Compounded Disadvantage: Race, Incarceration, and Wage Growth," *Social Problems* 58, no. 2 (2011), 257–280.

system and end the era of mass incarceration—and for the sake of the health and safety of our families and our communities, we must also support Americans returning home from prison and jail.

That's why we will:

- **Invest $5 billion in job programs with a proven record of success.** Formerly incarcerated individuals need support both before and after release to help them quickly navigate the challenges of workplace adjustment. To ensure they have a fighting chance at getting hired and succeeding in their first post-release job, we will invest $5 billion in job programs with a proven record of success. These programs help teach returning citizens how to network, excel in interviews, and answer difficult questions about their pasts. And when they are ready for work, they help them find and secure a stable job.

- **"Ban the box."** Many employers are reluctant to hire applicants with a criminal history, even if those applicants are capable and qualified. In a study of men in New York City, for example, a criminal record reduced the likelihood of a callback by almost 50 percent. However, research has found that employment prospects improve when applicants actually interact with a hiring manager—offering them a chance to display their qualifications before being asked about their criminal records.[38] We will take executive action to "ban the box" for federal employers and contractors so that applicants have a real opportunity to compete. We will require that any consideration of criminal history be job-related and that those rejected on the basis of criminal history receive both timely notice and the right to appeal.

---

38 "Research on Reentry and Employment," National Institute of Justice, 2016, http://www.nij.gov/topics/correc tions/reentry/pages/employment.aspx.

- **Restore voting rights to formerly incarcerated individuals.** We will support legislation that restores voting rights to individuals who served their sentences so they can fully participate in our democracy.

End the epidemic of gun violence.

Something is wrong in our country. There is too much violence, too much hate, too much senseless killing, and too many people dead who shouldn't be. An average of ninety people a day are killed by guns in the United States.[39] Gun violence is the leading cause of death for young African American men—more than the next nine leading causes combined.[40] It is time we do something about the gun violence epidemic that is sweeping across our communities and terrorizing our families.

The horrific tragedy in Orlando this year—the deadliest mass shooting in U.S. history—shed a bright light on the deep flaws in our country's gun laws. The Orlando gunman had previously been investigated by the FBI for having potential ties to terrorism—and yet he was able to legally purchase an assault rifle that he would later use to kill forty-nine

---

39   Sherry Murphy, Jiaquan Xu, et al., "Deaths: Final Data for 2013," *National Vital Statistics Reports* 64, no. 2 (2016), http://www.cdc.gov/nchs/data/nvsr/nvsr64/nvsr64_02.pdf.
40   "Leading Causes of Death Reports, National and Regional, 1999–2014: Search Black Males, Ages 15–24," Centers for Disease Control and Prevention, 2014, http://webappa.cdc.gov/sasweb/ncipc/leadcaus10_us.html.

Gun deaths:
How the U.S. stacks against other developed nations

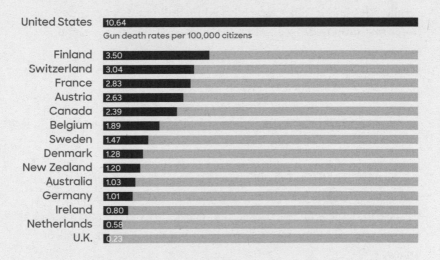

United States	10.64
	Gun death rates per 100,000 citizens
Finland	3.50
Switzerland	3.04
France	2.83
Austria	2.63
Canada	2.39
Belgium	1.89
Sweden	1.47
Denmark	1.28
New Zealand	1.20
Australia	1.03
Germany	1.01
Ireland	0.80
Netherlands	0.58
U.K.	0.23

Gun rates for Ireland, Australia, and France are 2012; Sweden, 2010; Canada, 2006; all other countries, 2011. Source: Centers for Disease Control and Prevention: GunPolicy.org

people without the sale being so much as flagged for the FBI.[41] Weapons of war like this one have no place on our streets, and we need comprehensive background checks to keep guns out of the wrong hands.

People on the terror watch list have tried to buy guns more than 2,400 times since 2005—and 90 percent of those purchases were successful. This is because the federal government currently does not prohibit suspected terrorists from buying firearms.[42] In 2007, the Bush administration proposed legislation to change that. The proposal—which has the support of more than two-thirds of gun owners—would allow the FBI to stop gun sales to known and suspected terrorists.[43] And yet the NRA and its allies have blocked the bill in every Congress since it was first proposed.[44] We will prioritize closing the "terror gap" once and for all.

> *We're not here to repeal the Second Amendment.*
> *We're not here to take away your guns.*
> *We just don't want you to be shot by somebody who shouldn't*
> *have a gun in the first place.*

Even if the FBI had the power to block gun sales to terror suspects, that alone would do little to stop terrorists from obtaining guns. That's because under federal law, background checks are only required for gun sales at brick-and-mortar stores—not purchases at gun shows or online.[45]

We are smart enough and strong enough as a nation to figure out how to protect the rights of responsible gun owners while keeping guns out of the hands of domestic abusers, gang members, other violent crimi-

---

41 Adam Goldman, Matt Zapotosky, and Mark Berman, "FBI had closely scrutinized the Orlando shooter before dropping investigation," *Washington Post,* June 13, 2016, https://www.washingtonpost.com/world/national-security/fbi-had-closely-scrutinized-the-orlando-shooter-before-dropping-investigation/2016/06/13/838e9054-3177-11e6-8ff7-7b6c1998b7a0_story.html.

42 Diana Maurer (GAO), written letter to Dianne Feinstein on NICS and Terrorist Watchlist Records, March 7, 2016, http://www.feinstein.senate.gov/public/index.cfm/files/serve?File_id=F53C4195-430D-4D8D-ACDE1EC53E97D0FA&SK=EF4E6FF4158FFA49E570234A3DE8E438.

43 "The Terror Gap," Center for American Progress, November 20, 2015, https://www.americanprogress.org/issues/guns-crime/report/2015/11/20/126060/fact-sheet-the-terror-gap/.

44 Lisa Masacaro and Jill Ornitz, "Senate votes down proposal to bar gun sales to terrorism suspects," *Los Angeles Times,* June 20, 2016, http://www.latimes.com/nation/la-na-gun-votes-20160620-snap-story.html.

45 "Federal Law on Private Sales," Law Center to Prevent Gun Violence, 2016, http://smartgunlaws.org/gun-laws/federal-law/gun-dealers-other-sellers/private-sales/.

nals, and the severely mentally ill. Despite all the political noise, Americans are actually united on this issue. The vast majority of Americans support comprehensive background checks. In fact, the conservative pollster Frank Luntz found that 82 percent of gun owners and 74 percent of NRA members support background checks for anyone buying a gun.[46] Democrats and Republicans overwhelmingly support them. As do leaders in law enforcement. So this isn't a matter of building popular support. We already have it. This is a matter of making elected officials do their jobs to keep our communities safe.

A good first step is closing the "Charleston Loophole" in our gun laws, which enables a person who is otherwise prohibited from buying a gun, such as a domestic abuser or other violent criminal, to buy one if their background check isn't completed within three business days.[47] This loophole allowed the alleged shooter at the Mother Emanuel AME Church in Charleston, South Carolina, to buy his gun despite his prior arrest record.[48]

And we will stand up to the gun lobby. Under an immunity law passed by a Republican-controlled Congress in 2005, victims of gun violence cannot legally hold irresponsible gun dealers or manufacturers accountable in most cases where their actions endanger Americans. Since the law was passed, nearly every lawsuit filed against gun manufacturers has been dismissed. The executive vice president of the NRA, Wayne LaPierre, has called the immunity law "the most significant piece of pro-gun legislation in 20 years."[49] We will repeal this law entirely and hold the gun industry accountable.

Now is not the time to be silenced or intimidated. As long as children anywhere are being killed by gun violence, we will keep fighting for our kids—because they deserve leaders who stand up for them, stand up to the gun lobby, and fight for real change.

---

46 "2012 Frank Luntz National Poll of Gun Owners and NRA Members," Everytown for Gun Safety Support Fund, October 20, 2012, https://everytownresearch.org/2012-polling-on-support-for-background-checks/.

47 "NICS Appeals," Criminal Justice Information Services, FBI, 2016, https://www.fbi.gov/services/cjis/nics/national-instant-criminal-background-check-system-nics-appeals.

48 Ellen Nakashima, "FBI: Breakdown in background check system allowed Dylann Roof to buy gun," *Washington Post,* July 10, 2015, https://www.washingtonpost.com/world/national-security/fbi-accused-charleston-shooter-should-not-have-been-able-to-buy-gun/2015/07/10/0d09fda0-271f-11e5-b72c-2b7d516e1e0e_story.html.

49 "President Bush Signs 'Protection of Lawful Commerce in Arms Act,' Landmark NRA Victory Now Law," NRA Institute for Legislative Action, 2005, https://www.nraila.org/articles/20051026/president-bush-signs-protection-of-br.

Break down the barriers that stand in the way of equal rights.

We will fight to break down all the barriers that hold Americans back and build ladders of opportunity for all of our people—so that every American can live up to his or her potential. That's the only way America can live up to its full potential, too.

We face a complex set of economic, social, and political challenges. They are intersectional, they are reinforcing, and we have to take them all on.

Our country's long struggle with racism is far from over. That's true in our criminal justice system, our education system, and in employment, housing, and transit. We have to see things as they are, not as we want them to be, and address systemic racism once and for all. Our schools are in the midst of a dangerous slide toward resegregation. Public schools today are actually more segregated now than they were in 1968. We have to fix that. The unemployment rate among young African Americans is twice as high as for young whites. We have to fix that, too.

Four decades after *Roe v. Wade*, women's fundamental right to make their own healthcare decisions is under concerted attack across the country. The majority of Americans believe women should have access to a safe and legal abortion. But in some states, a woman seeking reproductive health care will have to drive many hundreds of miles for an appointment. She may face a mandatory waiting period, or her doctor may be required to read her medically incorrect or misleading information prior to receiving an abortion. All of these restrictions can severely limit a woman's access to safe, quality health care. For instance, North Dakota has only one abortion clinic to serve more than 130,000 women of reproductive age.

Marriage equality is now the law of the land, but we still have a lot of work to do to ensure that all LGBT Americans are treated equally under the law. In many states, sexual orientation and gender identity are not protected under nondiscrimination statutes, putting people at risk of being fired from their jobs or refused an apartment rental because of who they are or who they love.

We have to take on all these challenges. Anything less just isn't good enough. When we invest in communities that have been left behind, and when we guarantee justice and dignity for every American, then we can truly make progress. We can build a future where no one is left out or left behind, and everyone can share in the promise of America.

We will:

- Secure environmental and climate justice
- Defend women's health and reproductive rights
- Demand equality for the LGBT community
- Protect and expand the rights of people with disabilities
- Fight HIV and AIDS
- End campus sexual assault
- Fight for equality for the people of Puerto Rico

Secure environmental and climate justice.

From Flint, Michigan, to Toledo, Ohio, to Charleston, West Virginia, families have been exposed to lead, dangerous algae, and toxic chemicals in their drinking water. Exposure to pesticides and chemicals has been linked to childhood cancer,[50] and the likelihood of such exposure can depend on where children live. For example, in the Manchester neighborhood of Houston, which is 85 percent Latino and where twenty-seven schools are within one mile of a high-risk chemical facility,[51,52] children who attend public schools are 56 percent more likely to get leukemia than those who live ten miles away.[53]

Simply put, this is environmental racism. And the impacts of climate change, from more severe storms to longer heatwaves to rising sea levels, will disproportionately affect low-income and minority communities, which suffer the worst losses during extreme weather and have the fewest resources to prepare.

Environmental and climate justice can't just be slogans—they have to be central goals. No one in our country should be exposed to toxic chemicals or hazardous waste simply because of where they live, their income, or their race. And the impacts of climate change must be addressed with an eye to climate justice, so no community gets left out or left behind.

That's why we will:

- **Eliminate lead as a major public health threat within five years.** Lead is a well-documented neurotoxin, and childhood lead exposure can irreversibly harm brain development, produce developmental delays, cause behavioral problems, and

---

50 Danielle Sedbrook, "2,4-D: The Most Dangerous Pesticide You've Never Heard Of," NRDC, March 15, 2016, https://www.nrdc.org/stories/24-d-most-dangerous-pesticide-youve-never-heard.
51 Emily Atkin, "How Houston's Biggest Polluters Are Buying Texas' Elections At The Expense Of Its Residents," *Think Progress,* October 29, 2014, http://thinkprogress.org/climate/2014/10/29/3584670/texas-elections-manchester/.
52 Vicki Wolf, "Houston: The Most Dangerous City," CLEAN, February 2014, http://www.cleanhouston.org/air/features/danger.htm.
53 Kristina M. Walker et al., "Epidemiologic Investigation—Executive Summary," The City of Houston, http://www.houstontx.gov/health/UT-executive.html.

negatively impact school performance. There is no safe blood-lead level in children. More than 535,000 children are poisoned by lead in the United States,[54] and children of color are more likely to be poisoned than white children.[55] We will establish a Presidential Commission on Childhood Lead Exposure and will direct every federal agency to adopt the commission's recommendations.

- **Create new economic opportunity through brownfield clean-up and redevelopment.** There are over 450,000 brownfield sites across the United States where the presence of hazardous substances, pollutants, and contaminants pose threats to public health and deprive local communities of economic development opportunities.[56] The EPA's Superfund program has insufficient resources to clean up the remaining sites on the National Priorities List, and most brownfields are overseen by capacity-constrained state and local governments.[57] We will work to replenish the federal Superfund, partner with state and local governments in pushing those responsible for pollution to pay their fair share of cleanup costs, and collaborate with local leaders to redevelop brownfields in a way that creates good-paying jobs and new economic opportunities for impacted communities.

54   William Wheeler and Mary Jean Brown, "Blood Lead Levels in Children Aged 1–5 Years—United States, 1999–2010," Centers for Disease Control and Prevention, April 5, 2013, http://www.cdc.gov/mmwr/preview/mmwrhtml/mm6213a3.htm.
55   Ibid.
56   "Brownfield Sites," Environmental Protection Agency, February 21, 2016, https://archive.epa.gov/pesticides/region4/landrevitalization/web/html/brownfieldsites.html.
57   Linda Breggin, Jay Pendergrass, and Keith Welks, "A Guidebook for Brownfield Property Owners," Environmental Law Institute, 1999, https://www.eli.org/sites/default/files/eli-pubs/d9.11.pdf.

- **Reduce urban air pollution by investing in clean power and transportation.** The United States has made important progress in reducing pollutants through cleaner power generation and more efficient cars and trucks. Yet in many communities, particularly communities of color, air pollution continues to threaten public health and safety.[58] More than 40 percent of Americans live in places where pollution levels are often too dangerous to breathe.[59] Urban air pollution contributes to asthma episodes, missed school and workdays, and reduced life expectancies for community residents. Through our Clean Energy Challenge, we will provide competitive grants that exceed federal standards and take the lead in deploying cost-saving and pollution-reducing clean energy and energy efficiency solutions. And we will defend and extend federal pollution standards for cars, trucks, and buses and invest in efficient transit that connects people to jobs and opportunity.

- **Broaden the clean energy economy, build career opportunities, and combat energy poverty.** We are committed to ensuring that no one is left behind or left out in the transition to a clean energy economy. We will ensure that the economic benefits of clean energy and energy efficiency are broadly shared. Our Clean Energy Challenge will help overcome barriers that prevent low-income families from reducing energy costs through solar panel installations and residential energy efficiency improvements. We will also work to expand good-paying job opportunities for people of color throughout the clean energy economy and help recruit and train workers from communities most heavily impacted by pollution. In today's economy African Americans hold only 1.1 percent of energy jobs and receive only 0.01 percent of energy sector profits.[60]

---

58   Michelle L. Bell and Keita Ebisu, "Environmental Inequality in Exposures to Airborne Particulate Matter Components in the United States," Environmental Health Perspectives, August 10, 2012, http://ehp.niehs.nih.gov/wp-content/uploads/2012/10/ehp.1205201.pdf.
59   "Key Findings for 2011–2013," American Lung Association, http://www.stateoftheair.org/2015/key-findings/.
60   Jacqui Patterson, "Just Energy Policies: Reducing Pollution and Creating Jobs," National Association for the Advancement of Colored People, December 2013, http://naacp.3cdn.net/5502c09b47ddedffb9_wrim6j5v0.pdf.

This has to change in the clean energy economy we build for the future.

- **Protect communities from the impacts of climate change by investing in resilient infrastructure.** Climate change will cause more frequent and severe downpours in the Northeast, potentially overwhelming aging drainage systems and causing sewage backups in predominantly low-income areas.[61] And sea level rise will threaten vulnerable communities from Baltimore to New Orleans.[62] More frequent and severe heat waves disproportionately threaten the health of people who can't afford adequate air conditioning or have preexisting health conditions.[63] State and local leaders are beginning to recognize the need to factor climate risks into infrastructure and public health planning and find creative solutions that protect their communities. We will give states and local communities the data, tools, and resources they need to make smart investments in resilient infrastructure and help diminish the local impacts of climate change.

---

61   "Climate Impacts in the Northeast," Environmental Protection Agency, February 23, 2016, https://www3.epa .gov/climatechange/impacts/northeast.html.
62   "Climate Impacts on Coastal Areas," Environmental Protection Agency, February 23, 2016, https://www3.epa .gov/climatechange/impacts/.
63   "Understanding the Link Between Climate Change and Extreme Weather," Environmental Protection Agency, February 23, 2016, https://www3.epa.gov/climatechange/science/extreme-weather.html.

Defend women's health and reproductive rights.

All women deserve to have their rights respected and to be guaranteed access to the health services and choices they are entitled to. Some politicians like to dismiss women's health and reproductive rights as "women's issues." Well, yes, these are women's issues. They are also family issues. They are economic issues. They are justice issues. And they are fundamental to our country and our future.

What's good for women is good for America. The percentage of women who finish college is six times what it was before birth control was legal.[64] Women now represent half of all college graduates in America and nearly half our labor force.[65] And the movement of women into the workforce over the past forty years was responsible for more than $3.5 trillion in growth in our economy.[66] As a result, our whole economy is better off.

But that has not stopped Republicans from trying time and time again to limit women's healthcare options. In just the first three months of 2016, states across the country introduced more than four hundred restrictions on abortion.[67] Planned Parenthood has been defunded in eleven states in the last year, cutting some women off from their primary healthcare provider.[68] And on a national level, Republicans in Congress have been willing to shut down the entire federal government to cut off Planned Parenthood funding.[69] Laws like the Hyde Amendment make it nearly impossible for low-income women, disproportionately women of color,[70] to exercise their full reproductive rights.

---

64   "Birth Control Has Expanded Opportunity for Women," Planned Parenthood, June 2015, https://www
.plannedparenthood.org/files/1614/3275/8659/BC_factsheet_may2015_updated_1.pdf.
65   "Women's Employment During the Recovery," United States Department of Labor, https://www.dol.gov/_sec/
media/reports/femalelaborforce/.
66   "How women can contribute more to the U.S. economy," McKinsey & Company, April 2011, http://www.mckinsey
.com/business-functions/organization/our-insights/how-women-can-contribute-more-to-the-us-economy.
67   Elizabeth Nash et al., "Trends in the States: First Quarter 2016," Guttmacher Institute, April 13, 2016, https://
www.guttmacher.org/article/2016/04/trends-states-first-quarter-2016.
68   The Editorial Board, "The State Assault on Planned Parenthood," *New York Times*, March 28, 2016, http://
www.nytimes.com/2016/03/28/opinion/the-state-assault-on-planned-parenthood.html?_r=0.
69   Amber Phillips, "How the Planned Parenthood debate could cause another government shutdown," *Washington Post*, August 4, 2015, https://www.washingtonpost.com/news/the-fix/wp/2015/08/04/how-the-planned-parenthood-debate-could-cause-a-another-government-shutdown/.
70   Jessica Arons and Lindsay Rosenthal, "How the Hyde Amendment Discriminates Against Poor Women and Women of Color," Center for American Progress, May 10, 2013, https://www.americanprogress.org/issues/women/news/2013/05/10/62875/how-the-hyde-amendment-discriminates-against-poor-women-and-women-of-color.

We cannot forget what life was like for women before *Roe v. Wade*—when women had far fewer options, and hundreds of women a year died as a result of botched, back-alley abortions.

Take Susan from Florida. Her grandmother—out of work and struggling to feed her two children—had an abortion on a kitchen table with no anesthetic, sterile equipment, or support. For weeks she had to worry about infection and getting arrested.

We know our country is freer, fairer, healthier, safer, and far more humane when women are empowered to make their own reproductive health decisions.

That's why we will:

- **Defend the fundamental right to safe and legal abortion.** Defending women's health means defending access to safe and legal abortion—not just in theory, but in reality. We know that restricting access doesn't make women less likely to end a pregnancy. It just makes abortion less safe—and threatens women's lives. Our administration will work to repeal the Hyde Amendment which makes it nearly impossible for low-income women to exercise their full reproductive rights. We also have to defend the progress we have made. America's maternal mortality rate dropped dramatically.[71] Our teen pregnancy rate is at its lowest point in two decades. And we must stand up for every woman in every state who has to miss work; drive hundreds of miles; endure cruel, medically unnecessary waiting periods; and walk past angry protesters to exercise her constitutional right to safe and legal abortion. We will fight to ensure every woman has more control, not less, over her health and future—and the right to safe and legal abortions is critical to that fight.

---

71 "Vital Statistics of the United States," Centers for Disease Control and Prevention, accessed July 2016, http://www.cdc.gov/nchs/products/vsus.htm.

- **Protect the Affordable Care Act and fight for women's preventive care, including access to affordable contraception.** The Affordable Care Act is the most significant advance for women's health in a generation. It bans insurance companies from discriminating against women and guarantees preventive care, including access to affordable contraception. Without the Affordable Care Act, 20 million Americans would lose their healthcare coverage, and insurance companies would be back in charge.[72] They would be free to discriminate against people with preexisting conditions—and free to go back to charging women more for health care than men.[73] We will not let the Affordable Care Act be repealed or weakened—we will defend and improve it.

- **Nominate Supreme Court justices who will defend women's rights.** Fifty-one years ago, the Supreme Court legalized birth control for married couples across America. Not long after that, *Roe v. Wade* guaranteed the right to safe, legal abortion. Being able to plan their families not only saved women's lives, it also transformed them—because it meant that women were able to get an education, build careers, enter new fields, and rise as far as their talent and hard work would take them. Some of the most important advancements in women's rights are thanks to the Supreme Court—but these accomplishments also remind us how much is at stake.

- **Fight back against attacks on Planned Parenthood and women's health and rights.** When Planned Parenthood was founded, women couldn't vote or serve on juries in most states. It was illegal even to provide information about birth control, let alone prescribe it. But now, Planned Parenthood

---

72 "20 million people have gained health insurance coverage because of the Affordable Care Act, new estimates show," Department of Health and Human Services, March 3, 2016, http://www.hhs.gov/about/news/2016/03/03/20-million-people-have-gained-health-insurance-coverage-because-affordable-care-act-new-estimates.
73 "The Affordable Care Act Helps Women," The White House, accessed July 2016, https://www.whitehouse.gov/sites/default/files/docs/the_aca_helps_women.pdf.

has provided essential services for over a century—mammograms, STD testing, sexual assault survivor care—and safe and legal abortion. Planned Parenthood should be funded, supported, and appreciated—not undermined, misrepresented, and demonized. We will fight to make sure the doors of Planned Parenthood remain open.

Protect and expand the rights of people with disabilities.

More than 50 million Americans are living with a disability, and for many years the issues that are important to their lives were ignored. Twenty-six years ago, Congress enacted the landmark Americans with Disabilities Act. It made our country more inclusive, our economy stronger, and our society fairer. The law and subsequent amendments have opened educational opportunities, expanded transportation, ensured equal access to public buildings, and outlawed employment discrimination on the basis of disability. The Supreme Court strengthened the rights of people with disabilities to live in integrated community settings in its decision in *Olmstead v. L.C.* Together, these changes have done so much to enable people with disabilities to participate fully in their communities and live the lives they want.

But our work in fully achieving that promise has just begun. That's why we will:

- **End the subminimum wage.** The subminimum wage has too often prevented people with disabilities from being treated fairly in the workplace and receiving the wages that others in their position would earn. In addition to raising the minimum wage, we need to make sure that people with disabilities can actually earn that wage for the work they do. This must be part of a broader effort to ensure that people with disabilities have access to competitive integrated employment so they, like others, can develop the skills they need to make a living in jobs that enable them to fully use their talents.

- **Enact the Disability Integration Act.** People with disabilities who receive long-term services and support should have a choice in how those services are delivered. We must improve opportunities for them to live in integrated community settings. This legislation would ensure that states and insurance providers offer home- and community-based services to anybody who needs long-term services and support and is eligible

218

for institutional-based care. This must also be part of a broader effort to ensure people with disabilities have better access and choice when it comes to housing.

- **Ratify the Convention on the Rights of Persons with Disabilities.** One hundred and sixty countries have signed this UN treaty protecting the rights and dignity of people with disabilities and guaranteeing them equal protections under the law. The Senate fell short of ratification the last time they considered this treaty, despite the vocal support of former Republican Senator Bob Dole. We will continue to push for the United States to join every other advanced economy by ratifying this treaty.

Demand equality for the LGBT community.

Thanks to the hard work of generations of LGBT advocates and activists who fought to make it possible, our country won a landmark victory in June 2015 when the Supreme Court recognized that in America LGBT couples—like everyone else—have the right to marry the person they love.

Marriage equality means Americans like Suzanne from Nashville, Indiana, can get married to the person they love. Suzanne married the love of her life at age sixty-seven—she and her wife were the first LGBT couple to marry in Brown County, Indiana. Their marriage should not have been so unique that it was filed away in the Indiana Historical Archives—but it was.

Our work to reach the promise of full equality remains unfinished. Nearly 65 percent of LGBT people report experiencing discrimination in their daily lives.[74] LGBT youth are nearly twice as likely as their peers to be physically assaulted at school,[75] and 74 percent of LGBT students say they've been verbally harassed for their sexual orientation.[76] And a recent study found that nearly 50 percent of LGBT elders experienced discrimination when applying for senior housing.[77] None of that takes into account the violence that goes unreported or ignored. Despite this discrimination, thirty-one states do not have fully inclusive LGBT nondiscrimination laws.[78] That means people can get married on a Sunday—and then are at risk of being fired or evicted because of their sexual orientation on Monday.

LGBT rights are human rights, and human rights are LGBT rights. No matter what we look like, where we come from, or who we are, we are all entitled to our human rights and dignity. We must stand firm and keep fighting until every American can not only marry, but also live, work, pray, learn, and raise a family free from prejudice and discrimination.

---

74 Brandon Lorenz, "New HRC Poll Shows Overwhelming Support for Federal LGBT Non-Discrimination Bill," Human Rights Campaign, March 17, 2015, http://www.hrc.org/blog/new-hrc-poll-shows-overwhelming-support-for-federal-lgbt-non-discrimination.
75 "Growing Up LGBT in America," Human Rights Campaign, June 7, 2012, http://www.hrc.org/youth-report.
76 Joseph G. Kosciw et al., "The 2013 National School Climate Survey," Gay, Lesbian & Straight Education Network, October 22, 2014, http://www.glsen.org/sites/default/files/2013%20National%20School%20Climate%20Survey%20Full%20Report_0.pdf.
77 "Opening Doors: An Investigation of Barriers to Senior Housing for Same-Sex Couples," Equal Rights Center, February 24, 2014, http://www.equalrightscenter.org/site/DocServer/Senior_Housing_Report.pdf.
78 "The 2016 Election: Know the facts about nondiscrimination protections," GLAAD, accessed July 2016, http://www.glaad.org/vote/topics/nondiscrimination-protections.

That's why we will:

- **Fight for full federal equality for LGBT Americans.** LGBT people still face discrimination in this country under the law. We cannot let it stand. We will work with Congress to pass the Equality Act, which would amend the Civil Rights Act of 1964 to add gender identity and sexual orientation to the list of protected classes such as race, sex, national origin, and religion. We will continue President Obama's LGBT equality executive actions including taking critical steps in employment, housing, and health care. And we will support efforts underway in the courts and federal government to clarify that under federal statutes "sex discrimination" includes discrimination on the basis of "gender identity" and "sexual orientation."

- **Support LGBT youth, parents, and elders.** LGBT youth face unique challenges at school and at home, LGBT parents face discriminatory barriers when attempting to start a family, and LGBT elders carry the consequences of a lifetime of discrimination into retirement. We will work to end discriminatory treatment of LGBT families in adoption to ensure that the estimated 108,000 children in foster care waiting to become part of loving families can be adopted by LGBT people.[79] For young LGBT people, we will improve school climates. We tell LGBT youth it gets better, but as a nation we have to do more to honor that promise. We will end so-called conversion therapy, the harmful practice of trying to "cure" LGBT and gender-questioning young people, because we should be providing LGBT kids with love, support, and compassion—not trying to change their identities. We will also combat youth homelessness. Some 40 percent of homeless youth identify as LGBT.[80] And we will ensure LGBT elders can retire with dignity and re-

---

79 "Meet the Children," Adopt US Kids, accessed July 2016, http://www.adoptuskids.org/meet-the-children.
80 Andrew Cray, Katie Miller, and Laura E. Durso, "Seeking Shelter: The Experiences and Unmet Needs of LGBT Homeless Youth," Center for American Progress, September 2013, https://www.americanprogress.org/wp-content/uploads/2013/09/LGBTHomelessYouth.pdf.

spect and are protected against discrimination. To better serve the LGBT community, we will collect national data on critical issues such as LGBT unemployment, health coverage, violence, and poverty by adding sexual orientation and gender identity to federally supported surveys.

- **Honor the military service of LGBT people.** Every day LGBT servicemembers valiantly fight for our country around the world. We believe we should honor their service and ensure they receive the benefits they have earned. That's why we will review and upgrade service records of LGBT veterans dismissed due to their sexual orientation before and during "Don't Ask, Don't Tell."

- **Protect transgender rights and end violence against the transgender community.** No one should be held back from fully participating in our society because of their gender identity. We must do more to end discrimination and violence against the transgender community. In 2015 alone, at least twenty-one transgender women—primarily, women of color—were murdered.[81] We need better data regarding crime victims and we will seek to improve reporting of hate crimes. We will also work to remove barriers to transgender Americans changing their gender marker on government IDs.

---

81   Hayley Miller, "Political Leaders Take Stand to Stop Anti-Transgender Violence," Human Rights Campaign, November 17, 2015, http://www.hrc.org/blog/political-leaders-take-stand-to-stop-anti-transgender-violence.

Fight HIV and AIDS.

The HIV and AIDS crisis in America began as a quiet, deadly epidemic—and because of discrimination and disregard, it remained that way for far too long. When many in positions of power turned a blind eye, activists, advocates, scientists, and heroic citizens fought with courage and compassion for a national commitment to combating the disease. There were all the people whose names we don't often hear today—the unsung heroes who fought on the front lines of the crisis, from hospital wards and bedsides, some with their last breath. Their courage—and their refusal to accept silence as the status quo—saved lives.

We've come a long way. The AIDS crisis looks very different today. The HIV-related mortality rate, which rose steadily through the 1980s, has declined by 85 percent since its peak in 1995.[82] There are more options for treatment and prevention than ever before. More people living with HIV are leading full and happy lives.

But HIV and AIDS continue to disproportionately impact communities of color, transgender people, young people, and gay and bisexual men. Today, roughly 1.2 million people in the United States are living with HIV.[83] Since the first case of AIDS was diagnosed in the United States in June 1981, more than 1.8 million people have been infected with HIV, and over 650,000 people have died.[84] Over the past decade, the number of new HIV infections has remained relatively unchanged, at roughly 50,000 new infections per year.[85]

We're still surrounded by memories of loved ones lost and lives cut short. But we're also surrounded by survivors who are fighting harder than ever. We owe it to them and to future generations to continue that fight together. For the first time, an AIDS-free generation is in sight. We will not let up until we reach that goal. We will not leave anyone behind.

---

82 "The HIV/AIDS Epidemic in the United States," Kaiser Family Foundation, April 7, 2014, http://kff.org/hivaids/fact-sheet/the-hivaids-epidemic-in-the-united-states/.
83 "HIV in the United States: At a Glance," Centers for Disease Control and Prevention, July 2015, https://www.cdc.gov/hiv/pdf/statistics_basics_ataglance_factsheet.pdf.
84 "The HIV/AIDS Epidemic in the United States," Kaiser Family Foundation.
85 Ibid.

That's why we will:

- **Work to fully implement the National HIV/AIDS Strategy.** The National HIV/AIDS Strategy provides an important roadmap in our march toward an AIDS-free generation. We will continue to implement the strategy and ensure a wide range of advocates and stakeholders are advising the Office of National HIV/AIDS Policy on execution.

- **Invest in research to end HIV and AIDS.** The AIDS crisis looks very different now than it did twenty years ago. Our nation's commitment to scientific research means that most people diagnosed with HIV today can live long lives with consistent treatment. Researchers at NIH and elsewhere are poised to make even more progress toward developing long-acting treatments and a cure for HIV. We will support robust investments to ensure this progress continues, and we will protect funding for this vital scientific research.

- **Cap out-of-pocket expenses for people living with HIV and AIDS.** It is an abomination that a pharmaceutical company can raise the price of medicine for HIV and AIDS patients by more than 5,000 percent.[86] Too many drug companies are gouging Americans with higher prices than they charge other people around the world. We will hold the pharmaceutical industry accountable and lower the cost of prescription drugs for Americans, including medications that help to prevent and treat HIV. We will cap monthly and annual out-of-pocket costs for prescription drugs at $250 and empower Medicare to negotiate lower drug prices. We will also end subsidies drug companies get for direct-to-consumer advertising and instead invest that money in research.

---

86   "CEO: 5,000-percent drug price hike 'not excessive at all,'" CBS News, September 22, 2015, http://www.cbsnews.com/news/turing-pharmaceuticals-ceo-martin-shkreli-defends-5000-percent-price-hike-on-daraprim-drug/.

- **Expand utilization of HIV prevention medications, including pre-exposure prophylaxis (PrEP).** PrEP and other medications have proved effective in preventing HIV infections and should be accessible to everyone. We will work to increase knowledge about and uptake of PrEP to ensure those at greatest risk of infection have access to the drug.

- **Fight to extend Medicaid coverage to provide lifesaving health care to people living with HIV.** Of the 70,000 people living with HIV who were uninsured before the Affordable Care Act, roughly 47,000 were supposed to be newly eligible for Medicaid.[87,88] However, the refusal of some states to expand Medicaid coverage means many of them still lack coverage. We will fight until every state expands Medicaid coverage to provide lifesaving health care to people living with HIV.

- **Reform outdated and stigmatizing HIV criminalization laws.** Discrimination should never be enshrined in our laws. We will work with advocates, HIV and AIDS organizations, Congress, and other stakeholders to review and reform outdated and stigmatizing federal HIV criminalization laws—and we will call on states to do the same. We will also continue to aggressively enforce the Americans with Disabilities Act and other civil rights laws to fight HIV-related discrimination.

---

87   "National HIV/AIDS Strategy for the United States: Updated to 2020," AIDS.gov, July 2015, https://www.aids .gov/federal-resources/national-hiv-aids-strategy/nhas-update.pdf.
88   Jennifer Kates and Rachel Garfield, "The ACA and People with HIV: The ACA's Impact and the Implications of State Choices," Health Affairs, March 3, 2014, http://healthaffairs.org/blog/2014/03/03/the-aca-and-people-with-hiv-the-acas-impact-and-the-implications-of-state-choices/.

End campus sexual assault.

It's not enough to condemn campus sexual assault. We need to end it. Sexual violence on campus is a crisis that demands action. An estimated one in five women report being sexually assaulted while in college.[89] We need to send a message to every survivor of sexual assault: You have the right to be heard, and you have the right to be believed. It's imperative that we provide confidential and comprehensive support to survivors, ensure a fair process for all involved, and increase sexual violence prevention education—not only in college, but also in secondary school.

We all need to be doing more to make it safe for everyone to receive an education without fear of sexual assault. The Obama administration has taken critical steps to address campus sexual assault. The President established a White House Task Force to Protect Students from Sexual Assault in 2014, and launched the "It's On Us" campaign, which emphasizes bystander intervention and outreach to young men. Vice President Biden introduced a new grant program to address the rape kit backlog, which affects sexual assault survivors on and off campus.

Our agenda builds on these reforms and addresses critical gaps in efforts to combat sexual assault. We all have a responsibility to address the scourge of sexual violence—on campuses, in our homes, on our streets, and in our communities.

That's why we will:

- **Provide comprehensive support to survivors.** Survivors of sexual assault on college campuses face enormous challenges, mentally and physically—they deserve all of our support. We need to make sure survivors are being taken care of with comprehensive services and treatment. To do that, we will ensure that every campus offers survivors the support they need—no matter their gender, sexual orientation, ethnicity, or race. Those

---

89 Michele C. Black et al., "The National Intimate Partner and Sexual Violence Survey: 2010 Summary Report," Centers for Disease Control and Prevention, November 2011, http://www.cdc.gov/ViolencePrevention/pdf/NIS-VS_Report2010-a.pdf.

services—from counseling to critical health care—should be confidential, comprehensive, and coordinated.

- **Ensure a fair process for all in campus disciplinary proceedings and the criminal justice system.** Too often the process of addressing a sexual assault on campus is confusing and convoluted. And many who choose to report in the criminal justice system fear that their voices will be dismissed instead of heard. We need a fair process for all involved, whether that's in campus disciplinary proceedings or in the criminal justice system. This includes providing all parties involved with notice and transparency in campus disciplinary proceedings, and ensuring that complaints filed in the criminal justice system are treated seriously.

- **Increase prevention efforts.** We need to recognize that it's not enough to address this problem by responding only once sexual assault occurs. We will reverse the tide by redoubling our prevention efforts and beginning those efforts earlier. We will increase sexual violence prevention education programs that cover issues like consent and bystander intervention—and we'll make sure we have programs not only in college, but also in secondary school.

Fight for equality for the people of Puerto Rico.

We know that Puerto Ricans want the same things as every American—the chance to live up to his or her God-given potential. Even that simple goal has often felt out of reach in Puerto Rico. For the last forty years, the island's economy has lagged behind the rest of the United States, and it has been in a deep recession for the last decade. Over the same period, the economy has shrunk by 20 percent. As a result, one out of every ten Puerto Ricans has moved to the mainland United States—and the island faces more hard times to come. The local government has been struggling to pay the tax refunds it owes its citizens and the payments it owes its suppliers.

Our citizens in Puerto Rico deserve a comprehensive plan to turn the economy around, and put its government on a path to sustainability.

First, federal officials must work with Puerto Rico's local self-government as laws are implemented and Puerto Rico's budget and debt are restructured so that it can get on a path toward stability and prosperity.

Second, we must recognize that the budget crisis is only one piece of the puzzle. Puerto Rico also needs a long-term plan to address its declining population, continuing job loss, high utility rates, and unequal federal investments. Puerto Rico's inconsistent treatment under federal laws has been a major factor in its economic decline. Let's start by equalizing funding for health care and support for families. Programs like Medicare, Medicaid, the Child Tax Credit, and the Earned Income Tax Credit can make a real difference when it comes to raising a family and earning a living. We will work hard to make sure equal access to these programs is guaranteed for Puerto Ricans.

Third, and most importantly, we will work as hard as we can with advocates from all sides of the issue to answer the fundamental question of Puerto Rico's political status. This decision is up to the people of Puerto Rico, and we commit to supporting their wishes. Any process to resolve Puerto Rico's legal status must be fair and consistent with the Constitution and laws of the United States, and the decision should be made by majority vote. We will support any process that meets these terms, such as an up or down vote on statehood. It's time to resolve this issue once and for all.

And of course, since Puerto Ricans are American citizens, we will fight for their right to vote in presidential elections.

Protect our environment and natural resources.

Last summer, for the first time since the 1970s, NASA published images of the Earth in a single frame. Taken one million miles away by a satellite, the images showed the "blue marble" shining bright against the vast blackness of space—a reminder of the beauty, fragility, and immeasurable value of our common home.

Our planet is facing new perils, climate change chief among them. Climate change is melting glaciers, eroding habitat, and diminishing water supplies. It is causing our seas to grow warmer and more acidic, damaging coral reefs that support entire ecosystems. Spring is coming earlier, summer burning hotter, and weather patterns shifting.

Americans pioneered the art and science of conservation, creating an unparalleled system of national parks and public lands and waters commonly called our "best idea." In past decades, we fought for clean air and clean water and for laws to protect endangered species. We created the Environmental Protection Agency and proved that we don't have to choose between protecting our environment and growing our economy— we can do both at the same time.

Now, we need to recommit ourselves to protecting our environment and leaving our children a better, safer, healthier world than the one we inherited. We need to develop an ethic of stewardship, responsibility, and sustainability in business, government, and in our own lives.

As we have described, we will make America a clean energy superpower and lead the global fight to combat climate change. We will secure environmental and climate justice for our most vulnerable citizens, because clean air and clean water are basic rights of all Americans, no matter where they live, what they look like, or how much money they have. And we will fight to protect our national parks, public lands and waters, and native species and hold them in trust for our children and grandchildren.

As Teddy Roosevelt said, "It is not what we have that will make us a great nation; it is the way in which we use it."

That's why we will:

- **Renew our shared commitment to conservation and keep our public lands public.** Our national parks, national forests, national seashores, wildlife refuges, and other public lands host more than 407 million visits every year. But America's parks— national, state, and local—are falling into disrepair and facing new pressures. Though they are more popular than ever, our national parks have an $11.5 billion maintenance backlog of aging roads, visitor centers, and infrastructure that need to be modernized, and the park system itself does not sufficiently include cultural and historic sites that reflect the diversity of our country. And too often, access to other public lands is restricted or at risk. Because national, state, and private lands are often intermixed, many hunters and anglers are finding locked gates and fences blocking access to publicly owned streams and wildlife habitat. Meanwhile, special interest groups are angling for the privatization of America's public lands, which would further reduce public access.

To meet these challenges, we will establish an American Parks Trust Fund with the mission of helping expand local, state, and national recreation opportunities, rehabilitate existing parks, enhance our great outdoors, and protect important wildlife habitats before they disappear. We will endeavor to tell the story of all Americans in our parks by doing more to represent communities of color, women, and LGBT Americans and diversify the public lands workforce. We will set a goal of unlocking access to at least 2 million acres of land that is currently inaccessible by the end of our first term. We will revitalize more than 3,000 city parks within a decade and protect and restore our nation's forests, including by working to protect and restore old growth forests and large landscapes that are essential to the health of our ecosystems. And above all, we will keep public lands public and fight special interest efforts to dispose of or sell off these national treasures.

- **Grow the outdoor economy and support working landscapes.** Hunting, fishing, hiking, and outdoor recreation contribute $646 billion annually to the U.S. economy and support 6.1 million American jobs. Recent studies have found that communities with accessible outdoor recreation opportunities experience a competitive advantage, as new businesses and workers relocate to these areas. Conserving our nation's lands, waters, and oceans not only protects our natural heritage, it improves quality of life and creates new jobs and economic opportunity. Partnering with private landowners, ranchers, and farmers can achieve conservation goals and strengthen rural economies. That's why we will set a goal of doubling the size of the outdoor economy within a decade.

To get it done, we will expand Small Business Administration assistance for entrepreneurs looking to launch small businesses in the outdoor industry and designate outdoor recreation clusters where the government can work in partnership with community and business leaders to improve outdoor recreation infrastruc-

ture and attract new visitors, businesses, and workers.
We will also encourage the sound stewardship of our working
landscapes, including farms, ranches, and privately owned
forests. These lands are critical to the economic health of our
rural communities and our environment. We will incentivize
voluntary conservation of lands, waters, and species habitat, and
make it easier for farmers and ranchers to identify and apply
for programs that could support their conservation practices.

- **Expand clean-energy production on public lands and waters
tenfold and reform leasing.** Offshore wind in public waters has
the potential to meet up to 20 percent of our nation's electricity
demand. Onshore, public lands appropriate for development
have untapped potential for solar, wind, biomass, and geother-
mal energy. We will streamline permitting for these projects,
do more to build efficient transmission lines to get low-cost
renewable energy to market, and work across federal agencies to
make sure these investments are benefiting local communities.
And we will reform our fossil fuel leasing practices. Our administration will oppose offshore leasing in the Arctic and the
Atlantic. And we will reform onshore leasing to ensure taxpayers are getting a fair deal; raise royalty rates, which currently lag
below the rates on state and private lands; and close loopholes
to make sure production is happening as safely as possible.

4.

WORKING TOGETHER

Breaking Through the Gridlock to Get Results

Democratic National Convention—Philadelphia, Pennsylvania, July 28, 2016.

IF YOU'VE READ THIS FAR (and thank you for that!), you're probably thinking, well, that all sounds pretty good, but how are you going to get it done?
How are you going to break through the gridlock in Washington?

We get that. We understand why so many Americans are cynical
about our political system. Our campaign finance laws allow the wealthy
and big corporations to drown out the voices of everyday Americans.
Too many policymakers in Washington are more beholden to special
interests, from the gun lobby to the oil lobby, than they are to the interests of their constituents. In recent years, Republicans in Congress have
been more interested in defeating the President than in advancing our
country, and as a result, we've had two of the least-productive Congresses
in our history. And too many states are making it harder for Americans,
particularly young people, low-income people, the elderly, and people of
color, to access the ballot box in the first place.

This is the greatest democracy in the history of the world. We
should be protecting people's right to vote, not corporations' right to buy
elections. We must remember we are stronger together.

We're going to start by curbing the outsize influence of big money
in American politics, because we know that voters will have a hard time
believing Washington will work for them otherwise. We have to end the

flood of secret, unaccountable money that is distorting our elections, corrupting our political system, and drowning out the voices of too many Americans.

That begins with immediately fighting to overturn *Citizens United*. Decided by the U.S. Supreme Court in 2010, the *Citizens United* case helped unleash hundreds of millions of dollars of secret, unaccountable money into our elections. *Citizens United* was a wrongheaded decision, but the Supreme Court has been limiting our ability to regulate America's campaign finance system since *Buckley v. Valeo* was decided in 1976. In that case, the Court equated money with speech, laying the groundwork for decades of decisions overturning commonsense campaign finance limits in courts across the country.

To establish commonsense rules to protect against the undue influence of billionaires and special interests, we must amend the Constitution to overturn *Citizens United*. We will introduce an amendment to do that within our first thirty days in office. And we will appoint Supreme Court justices who value people's right to vote over billionaires' rights to buy elections.

We also need to do more to make sure that candidates and elected officials are spending their time listening to constituents, not dialing for dollars. Our campaign finance system is full of perverse incentives that keep those with good ideas but few political connections from seeking elective office and serving the country, especially women and people of color. That's why we will establish a small-donor matching system for presidential and congressional candidates that will provide multiple matching funds for small donations, increasing small donors' role and influence and making it easier for working Americans who aren't wealthy or well-connected to run for office.

We believe the public has a right to know who is spending money to influence elections and the actual sources of funds for those expenditures. That's why we will push for legislation to require outside groups to publicly disclose significant political spending, and promote SEC rulemaking to require publicly traded companies to disclose all political spending to their shareholders. If Congress fails to act on commonsense campaign finance reform, we will sign an executive order requiring federal government contractors to fully disclose all political spending.

But campaign finance reform is only one piece of the equation. There is a sweeping effort underway across our country to disempower and disenfranchise people of color, poor people, and young people at the voting booth.[1]

Since the Supreme Court eviscerated a key provision of the Voting Rights Act in 2013, many of the states that previously faced special scrutiny because of a history of racial discrimination have proposed and passed new laws that make it harder than ever to vote. [2]

North Carolina, for example, passed a bill that went after virtually everything that makes voting more convenient or more accessible, including early voting, same-day registration, and voter outreach programs. in high schools.[3] A U.S. Appeals court recently struck the law down, citing the "almost surgical precision" with which the law targeted and disenfranchised African American voters. Under Texas's voter ID law, a concealed weapon permit is a valid form of identification, but a student ID is not.[4] In South Carolina, there is supposed to be one voting machine for every 250 voters.[5] But in communities of color, this rule is often not followed, causing long lines and massive delays to cast a ballot.[6] And nationwide, voters of color are more likely than white voters to wait in long lines at polls.[7]

---

1   Andrew Cohen, "How Voter ID Laws Are Being Used to Disenfranchise Minorities and the Poor," *Atlantic*, March 16, 2012, http://www.theatlantic.com/politics/archive/2012/03/how-voter-id-laws-are-being-used-to-disenfranchise-minorities-and-the-poor/254572/; and Susan Milligan, "I (Wish I) Voted: Recent changes to voting rights impact elections," *U.S. News & World Report*, April 1, 2016, http://www.usnews.com/news/the-report/articles/2016-04-01/voting-restrictions-are-impacting-elections.

2   Tomas Lopez, "Shelby County: One Year Later," Brennan Center for Justice at New York University School of Law, June 24, 2014, http://www.brennancenter.org/analysis/shelby-county-one-year-later.

3   Alan Blinder and Richard Fausset, "Federal Judge Upholds North Carolina Voter Rules," *New York Times*, April 25, 2016, http://www.nytimes.com/2016/04/26/us/politics/federal-judge-upholds-north-carolina-voter-id-law.html.

4   Rebecca Leber, "In Texas, You Can Vote With a Concealed Handgun License—but not a Student ID," *New Republic*, October 20, 2014, https://newrepublic.com/article/119900/texas-voter-id-allows-handgun-licenses-not-student-ids.

5   Christopher Famighetti, Amanda Melillo, and Myrna Perez, "Election Day Long Lines: Resource Allocation" (New York: Brennan Center for Justice at New York University School of Law, 2014), accessed July 27, 2016,: http://www.brennancenter.org/sites/default/files/publications/ElectionDayLongLines-ResourceAllocation.pdf.

6   The Editorial Board, "Long Lines at Minority Polling Places," *New York Times*, September 24, 2014, http://www.nytimes.com/2014/09/25/opinion/long-lines-at-minority-polling-places.html?_r=0.

7   Jeremy W. Peters, "Waiting Times at Ballot Boxes Draw Scrutiny," *New York Times*, February 4, 2013, http://www.nytimes.com/2013/02/05/us/politics/waiting-times-to-vote-at-polls-draw-scrutiny.html.

While controversial state laws like these get most of the attention, many of the worst offenses against the right to vote happen below the radar.

Authorities can shift poll locations and election dates, or scrap language assistance for non-English speakers. Without the preclearance provisions of the Voting Rights Act, no one outside the local community is likely to ever hear about these abuses, let alone have a chance to challenge them and end them.

Every citizen has the right to vote. And we should be doing everything we can to make it easier for citizens to vote, not harder.

That is why we will fight to restore the full strength of the Voting Rights Act and restore the full protections American voters need and deserve. Yes, this is about democracy. But it's also about dignity—about the right of every person, no matter their age, race, or socioeconomic status, to be able to stand up and say, "I am an American, and my voice counts."

But that's not enough. We need to make it easier for eligible voters to exercise their fundamental right to vote. That is why we will fight to ensure that every citizen, in every state, is automatically registered to vote when they turn eighteen, unless they actively choose to opt out. We will also work to make sure registration rolls are secure, up-to-date, and complete, and that when a voter moves, his or her registration moves, too.

And we will expand opportunities to vote. We will work to set a new national standard of no fewer than twenty days of early, in-person voting, including opportunities for evening and weekend voting, and establish the principle that no one should have to wait more than thirty minutes to cast their ballot. Early, in-person voting will reduce long lines and give more citizens the chance to participate, especially those who have work or family obligations that make it difficult to get to the polls on Election Day. Expanding early voting is not just convenient—it's also more secure, more reliable, and more affordable than absentee voting.

We are stronger when everyone has a say in the direction of our country—and when we don't cede our public discourse to whoever can afford to buy the biggest megaphone.

We need to figure out new ways to work across the aisle, too. We both have long records of bipartisanship. We both believe that even if you are 100 percent right, to get something done you still need to compromise with those who don't agree with you. That doesn't mean you abandon your principles by any means. But it does mean that you make progress, you have to be open to hearing others' opinions and really try to understand where they are coming from.

If there's a common theme in every chapter of the American story, it's Americans from all backgrounds coming together to find common ground and make a difference.

Amid a struggle against one of the world's greatest empires, delegates from thirteen squabbling colonies gathered in Philadelphia to debate their future. The colonies had separate economies, cultures, and politics. John Adams called the Continental Congress a "gathering of strangers." Our founders knew that our nascent nation could only survive if everyone from New Hampshire to Georgia pulled together. As we've noted earlier in these pages, they overcame deep disagreements to find common ground for the sake of their shared future.

They quickly realized they could no longer be strangers—they needed to be countrymen. So they put aside their disagreements and declared independence as the United States of America, promising to "mutually pledge to each other our Lives, our Fortunes and our sacred Honor."

A decade later, delegates from across the continent gathered again in Philadelphia. This time, they needed to decide how tightly the states wanted to tie themselves to one another. The loose association drawn up during the revolution was no longer working. States were acting like independent nations, competing with one another and looking out only for their own self-interest. Once again, the thirteen states, which had so recently been colonies, agreed that the way forward was to tie themselves more closely together. In Philadelphia, the founders wrote our Constitution—with the goal of forming "a more perfect union."

The patriots in Philadelphia realized they were all going to rise or fall together—and decided they would be stronger together. More than two hundred years later, that's still true. Every generation since our founding has fought to expand the circle of opportunity, prosperity, and freedom ever wider, and build a better and brighter future for those who follow us.

We all have a role to play in the march of progress, in the hard and often frustrating work of building that more perfect union. Making a difference in people's lives isn't a Democratic priority or a Republican priority—it's an American priority. We all rise together when there are more good-paying jobs, more children lifted out of poverty, and all Americans have what Abraham Lincoln called "a fair chance in the race of life."

Too many in Washington have forgotten that. Rather than finding common ground to move the country forward, Republicans in Congress have lurched from crisis to crisis, even shutting the government down. Even legislation to invest in our nation's infrastructure—for decades an issue where the parties could come together—has fallen victim to gridlock. Working across party lines is looked down on, not lifted up as a model.

That's not the way America is supposed to work. Like our founding leaders in Philadelphia, we need to pull together, bridge our differences, and come up with real solutions.

We'll sweat the details and be specific.
We care about the exact level of lead in the drinking water in Flint.
We care about how much your child's asthma inhaler costs.
We care about the interest rate you're paying on your student loans.
Because when it's your child, your water, your bills,
these aren't details, they're a big deal,
they should be a big deal to your leaders.

Here's how we'll get things done for the American people.

We'll start by listening. We think it's pretty simple: You can't help solve problems if you don't understand what they are. Americans shouldn't have to scream to be heard. The American people deserve a President and a Vice President who understand not only the big challenges we need to tackle as a country—creating millions of good-paying jobs, combating terrorism, tackling climate change—but the quiet problems that keep families up at night.

Second, we'll roll up our sleeves and come up with smart solutions that will make a real difference in people's lives. We'll sweat the details and be specific. We care about the exact level of LEAD in the drinking water in Flint. We care about how much your child's asthma inhaler costs. We care about the interest rate you're paying on your student loans. Because when it's your child, your water, your bills, these aren't details, they're a big deal—and they should be a big deal to your leaders.

And we believe you deserve to know what we will do, how we will pay for it, and how we will get it done. That's why we wrote this book—so you would understand our plans for growing the economy, keeping our country safe, and breaking down all the barriers that hold Americans back.

Finally, we will work hard to turn those plans into reality. Getting results means working with all types of players—from members of Congress of both parties to policy experts to advocates and activists—to reach agreement. And getting results means understanding that compromise is not a bad thing. Major accomplishments like the Voting Rights Act, the Clean Air and Clean Water Acts, Social Security, Medicare, Medicaid all needed votes from both parties to become law.

And if we aren't able to find common ground, we won't hesitate to do the right thing using our executive authority—as President Obama has done to protect DREAMers from deportation, tackle climate change, and raise wages for federal contractors. That's what it means to be progressives who like to get things done.

In today's hyper-partisan world, some wonder if it's really possible to come together to solve big, contentious issues—from reforming our broken immigration system to finally achieving universal health care to making a college education debt-free for all.

It won't be easy. And yes, it'll take time. But if we come together, there's nothing we can't accomplish.

Making Progress Starts by Listening
Hillary Clinton

When I was First Lady, I fought tooth and nail to pass universal health care. The insurance companies and other special interests defeated our effort to get health insurance for every American, but I didn't give up. I had heard from so many parents of children with chronic illnesses, or who had survived acute health issues like cancer, who couldn't find insurance at any price. I still remember meeting one father at Children's Hospital in Cleveland. He owned his own business, and provided health insurance for his employees and their families, but no one would insure his two children with cystic fibrosis. He had one insurance salesman explain his refusal to sell him coverage by saying "You don't understand. We don't insure burning houses." They called his little girls, the lights of his life, "burning houses."

So I worked with Democrats and Republicans to create the Children's Health Insurance Program, which covers children from families who can't afford private insurance but earn too much to be covered by Medicaid. At the time, it was the largest expansion of public health insurance coverage since Medicaid was created in 1965. Although I couldn't vote for it, Senator Ted Kennedy made my role pretty clear: "The children's health program wouldn't be in existence today if we didn't have Hillary pushing for it from the other end of Pennsylvania Avenue." Today, CHIP covers more than 8 million children.

You see, it's important to stand your ground and fight for what you believe in. But sometimes the only way to make progress is to find common ground with those who don't agree with you on much. Then-House Majority Whip Tom DeLay was one of the most vocal critics of my husband's administration and the Democratic agenda. But I learned he was a foster parent. And it turned out that we both had some ideas for how we could improve the foster care system and make it easier for foster kids of all ages to get adopted.

So we got to work on the Adoption and Safe Families Act to help kids find adoptive families and keep them from "aging out" of the system when they turn eighteen. I still get letters from parents who were able to adopt their children because of the law Tom DeLay and I worked on together.

My experiences working with Republicans and Democrats to chart a path forward on children's issues when I was First Lady prepared me well for my time in the Senate. In fact, I worked with almost every one of my Republican colleagues during my eight years in Congress. Sometimes I cosponsored their legislation, sometimes they cosponsored mine. South Carolina Republican Lindsey Graham and I worked together to expand healthcare coverage for reservists in the National Guard, so they wouldn't lose coverage when they weren't on active duty. Arizona Republican John McCain and I worked together to get more help for soldiers with traumatic brain injuries. There was a lot we didn't agree on—but I worked hard to find common ground wherever I could.

My first job out of college was for the Children's Defense Fund, going door-to-door in New Bedford, Massachusetts, on behalf of children with disabilities who were denied the chance to go to school. We interviewed children and parents, gathered facts, built a coalition—and our work helped convince Congress to guarantee access to education for all students with disabilities. It's a big idea—and to make it real, we had to go step-by-step, year by year, even door by door.

Simply caring is not enough. To drive real progress you have to change both hearts and laws. You need both understanding and action. And if I have the honor of serving as President, that's how we'll make change happen for the American people.

———————

If You Want to Do Right, Be an Optimist
Tim Kaine

My parents taught me early lessons that have guided my life: The importance of hard work, of faith and kindness, of following your dreams. My mom once told me, "Tim, you have to decide whether you want to be right or you want to do right. If you want to be right, go ahead and be a pessimist. But if you want to do right, be an optimist." I've been an optimist ever since.

I got my start as a city council member and mayor building schools, cutting crime, and creating jobs. That experience has helped me keep my focus on what really matters to people. When I was governor of Virginia, we were facing the worst economic crisis since the Great Depression. We had to make a lot of tough choices. But we still managed to work on a bipartisan basis to expand early education, build more classrooms, and expand our college campuses so more people could enroll—because education is the key to everything we wanted to achieve as a state, and key to everything parents want for their kids.

April 16, 2007, was the worst day of my life. I had just arrived in Japan on a trade mission and gone to sleep when I got a knock on my door. A shooting at Virginia Tech had killed thirty-two students and professors, from eighteen-year-old freshmen to a Holocaust survivor in his seventies, a teacher who blocked the door of his classroom with his body so his students could get away. I flew straight home to Virginia.

In the weeks that followed, we learned how the shooter had been able to get a gun despite the fact that he should have been prohibited because of severe, legally documented mental health issues. But the system didn't work the way it was supposed to. That's why I stood up to the gun lobby and signed an executive order to close the gaps in Virginia's background-check system.

We fought for more reforms that ultimately didn't pass—but I remain committed to taking action to prevent gun violence, including by finally getting comprehensive background checks in place and closing loopholes that allow guns to fall into the hands of people who should not have them.

I took my local and state experience with me to the Senate. It's more important than ever that people continue their educations after high school—but you shouldn't have to go to a four-year college to be able to live a middle-class life. That's why I've made expanding opportunities for career and technical education a focus, fighting to make sure that federal education policy recognizes the value of career and technical education, getting states to track these efforts, and expanding funding for high-quality programs. And I have also fought for strong national defense, strong diplomacy, and jobs for veterans.

And I have worked hard to reach across the aisle. In fact, I worked with Republican Senators—including Lindsey Graham, Jeff Flake, Kelly Ayotte, and Susan Collins—to write a bill to block suspected terrorists from being able to buy guns. We haven't been able to break through opposition to pass the bill yet, but I take heart in the knowledge that we can find common ground across party lines on preventing gun violence.

When I was growing up, my favorite President was Harry Truman. Truman said that America was not built on fear, but on courage, on imagination, and an unbeatable determination to do the job at hand. These are tough times for many in our country, but we're tough people. And while tough times don't last, tough people do.

I'm one of only about thirty people in American history to serve as a mayor, a governor, and a U.S. senator. That means I have been able to see how government works, and how sometimes it doesn't, from just about every perspective. I've always believed that however you serve, what matters is whether you actually deliver results for people. That's been my goal in every position I've ever held, and that will be my goal if I have the privilege of serving as Vice President.

———————

Good ideas aren't Democratic or Republican—they're just good ideas. No matter the problem, there is someone somewhere in America working to solve it. The trick is to find those leaders who are making real change happen on the ground, find ways to support them so they can do even more, and make them an example for the rest of the country to follow.

Our mayors know that it doesn't matter if a Democrat or a Republican fixes the problem—it just needs to be fixed. It's much harder to punt on an issue when the person struggling is your next-door neighbor. That's why so many innovative solutions to the challenges we face are coming from states and local communities.

Denver is building a twenty-first-century transit system that will keep the city moving and growing for generations to come.

Oklahoma City is investing in parks, bike trails, and sidewalks to keep families healthy.

Compton is helping people get construction jobs rebuilding their own neighborhoods.

Williamson, West Virginia, is working to create jobs and improve health care in a community ravaged by the loss of mining jobs.

Miami Beach, on the front lines of climate change, is investing in resilient infrastructure and sounding the alarm for other cities.

New York City is expanding preschool so every four-year-old gets a good start in life.

New Orleans has invested in proven solutions, like permanent supportive housing, to bring an end to veteran homelessness.

And states are making change happen, too. California and Washington are leaders in the fight against climate change, deploying new clean energy solutions, investing in energy efficiency, and pioneering new ways of doing business. New York raised the minimum wage. Connecticut passed a paid family leave bill.

What all of these leaders need is a federal government that supports them as they work to make change happen. That's why many of our proposals follow what we call a "flexible federalism" model. We want to set big goals and strong standards, and give states and cities the space they need to find solutions that work for them. That's how we'll get to 500 million solar panels by the end of our first term. It's how we'll take on the epidemic of addiction. It's how we'll get college costs under control and work with states to reinvest in higher education. And we will do more to work with nonprofits and community-minded businesses—because this is an all-hands-on-deck time, and we need everyone working together.

So we will push to expand the New Markets Tax Credit program to cover more communities and provide even stronger assistance than it does today. This is a tax credit that supports economic revitalization efforts in hard-hit communities and has made a difference in all fifty states. We will steer more funding to the communities that have struggled the hardest and longest, using approaches like the 10-20-30 plan, pioneered by South Carolina Representative Jim Clyburn in the Recovery Act. The idea is simple: to direct 10 percent of program dollars to communities where 20 percent or more of people have lived in poverty for 30 years, because those neighborhoods where we have generational poverty need extra help to be able to get themselves up and moving forward.

We are facing real challenges as a country. Too many families feel like the economy isn't working for them. Too many people are frustrated—even furious. And they're right. Our economy isn't working the way it should. Our politics isn't delivering results the way it should. And there is still too much inequality and distrust in our society. We still have work to do to secure our rights—civil rights and voting rights, women's rights and workers' rights, LGBT rights and rights for people with disabilities.

Every generation of Americans has come together to make our country freer, fairer, and stronger. None of us ever have or can do it alone. We know that at a time when so much seems to be pulling us apart, it can be hard to imagine how we'll ever pull together. But progress is possible. America's destiny is ours to choose—and we choose to be stronger together.

(Left to right) Anne Holton, President Clinton, Tim Kaine, and Hillary Clinton at a rally in downtown Harrisburg, Pennsylvania, July 29, 2016.

Whatever party you belong to—
or if you belong to no party at all—
if you share our belief that America is stronger together,
this is your campaign.

If you believe we should build
an economy that works for everyone,
not just those at the top,
join us.

If you believe that we should say "no"
to unfair trade deals
and support our steelworkers, our autoworkers,
and our homegrown manufacturers,
join us.

If you believe that every man, woman, and child
in America has the right to affordable health care,
join us.

If you believe that your working mother,
wife, sister, or daughter deserves equal pay,
join us.

If you believe unity is better than division,
that bridges are better than walls,
and that America's best days are still ahead of us—
join us.

Go to
hillaryclinton.com/events
to find out more about volunteer
opportunities in your area.

HILLARY CLINTON served as the sixty-seventh Secretary of State—from January 21, 2009, until February 1, 2013—after nearly four decades in public service advocating on behalf of children and families as an attorney, First Lady, and Senator.

TIM KAINE is a United States Senator for Virginia. A former missionary and civil rights attorney, he is one of only thirty people to have served as Mayor, Governor, and Senator.